Gold Dust

How to become a more effective coach, quickly

David and Keith Mayer

Table of Contents

Dedication to Dick Bate – by Keith Mayer 1

Thank You 3

Introduction - What is Gold Dust About? 5

Where Did Gold Dust Start? – by Keith Mayer 6

What is a Coach? 7

Enjoy Your Journey 8

Chapter 1 - The Lone Wolf: The Story of a Boy
– An experience from Keith Mayer 11

Listen Purely, Explore Deeply 19

Chapter 2 - Building a Connection 21

Know Yourself First 21

Building Rapport 22

Pace Before You Lead 24

Possess A Genuine Warmth 27

Use the Athlete's Name 30

Do Your Homework 33

Chapter 3 - Building on the Connection 35

What is Coaching? 36

The Journey 38

Understand the Level of the Relationship 39

Alignment 40

Harmony 42

Behavioural Changes 44

Ask Good Questions 45

The Influencer Relationships 46

Make Them Feel Good 48

Chapter 4 - Gaining and Maintaining Motivation................... 49

What is Motivation?.. 49

Intrinsic and Extrinsic Motivation 50

"Towards" and "Away From" Motivation 50

Understanding the Athletes Motivations................................. 51

An Individual's Expectations... 52

Reframing 53

Breaking Self-Limiting Beliefs... 54

Providing Evidence 56

Chunking.. 56

Chunking Up 57

Chunking Down 57

Chunking Across.. 57

Understanding the Importance of Chunking............................ 58

Chapter 5 - The Highly Effective Coach 59

Process Over Content... 59

The Storyteller 60

Anchor the Feelings 61

Be Mindful of Your Thoughts 62

Pattern Interrupts.. 64

The Art of Observation 65

Be Aware of Mind Reading... 67

Situational Understanding... 68

Be Mindful of Other Interactions.. 71

The Power of Unspoken Words 71

The Power of Notes 72

The Mavericks and Master Locksmiths..................................... 73

Chapter 6 - The Highly Effective Communicator....................**75**

The Use of Your Words.. 75

    Embed Commands 75

    Embed Questions 76

    The Use of If.. 76

    The Use of But... 77

    The Benefit of Providing Options 79

    The Power of Agreement 80

    Ask Questions to Get Permission 80

    Speak to Individuals Within a Group.............. 81

    White Noise 83

The Use of Your Voice 84

    Volume 87

    Pace 87

    Pitch 88

    Breathe and Pause 88

Be Aware of Your Body Language............................ 88

    Coach Energy 89

Chapter 7 - Effective Praise **91**

Praise Effort, Especially in Children....................... 93

Know Who You're Praising 96

Be Specific with Your Praise................................... 97

Consistent Mindsets 99

Environmental Differences 100

Chapter 8 - The Silent Whisperer................................. **103**

How Can You Be A Silent Whisperer? 104

Whisper to Outside Influences 105

Whisper with Situational Awareness....................... 105

Whisper to Your Inner Circle 106

Creating Other Whisperers... 108

Whispering Through Notes.. 110

Chapter 9 - Thank Your Athlete **111**

Chapter 10 - Minister of Care.................................... **115**

A Little Gesture Can Go a Long Way 117

Come Dine with Me 117

Protect Your Athletes 117

Care About the Wellbeing of Your Athletes 118

Chapter 11 - The 21ˢᵗ Century Coach....................... **123**

Your Learning Process 124

Be Curious 126

Evolving and Adapting 128

Influence with Integrity.. 130

Communicate Effectively 132

Utilise Your Mentors... 133

Chapter 12 - The Conclusion

– Be Like The Master Boilermaker **137**

The Boilermaker Story... 137

About The Authors **141**

References **143**

Dedication to Dick Bate – by Keith Mayer

This book is dedicated to my close friend, Dick Bate. The footballing circle lost a pioneer, a maverick and one of the finest coach educators the World has seen when Dick passed away in April 2018. The thousands of coaches that had the pleasure to observe his captivating sessions were in the presence of greatness. His sessions were constantly filled with unparalleled technical detail that always ignited the imagination of those present.

Whenever Dick and I spoke, he always inspired me with this ability to make me feel special. He was a mentor, and a friend. Dick has played a huge part in my life, and for that, I will be forever grateful. I miss our conversations my friend.

In dedication to Dick, 10% of profits from this book will be donated to The Giles' Trust, the brain tumour fund within the University Hospital Birmingham Charity.

Thank You

The making of this book would not have been possible without those that helped shape the views and beliefs that are shared in this book, especially Dr. Richard Bandler, a genius in the fields of behaviour change, the art of communication and personal development. He is the finest teacher the world may ever see, and we have been lucky to be in his presence and learn from him.

We would also like to thank all of coaches mentioned below who contributed to the book with their stories, experiences and ideas. There are hundreds of years combined experience in coaching and dealing with people across different sports featured in the book. Their help has been greatly appreciated in this process. In first name alphabetical order:

Chris Millington – Assistant Manager at FC Halifax Town.

Darren Moore – Current Doncaster Rovers FC Manager. Ex-Premier League footballer and ex West Brom Manager in the Premier League.

Gareth Holmes – Professional Phase Lead Coach at Nottingham Forest.

Justin Holbrook – Gold Coast Titans Rugby League Head Coach. One of the most successful Super League coaches of all time as Head Coach at St Helens RLFC.

Kevin Harper – Former 2x Thai Boxing World Champion. Owns a combat a gym with boxing, MMA and Thai Boxing with over 50 Champions, including several World Champions.

Mick Beale – Current Rangers FC First Team Coach. Ex professional footballer. Previously coached at Chelsea FC, Liverpool FC and Sao Paolo as Assistant Manager.

Nick Marshall – Current Assistant Academy Manager and Head of Coaching at Liverpool FC. Ex Academy Manager at Nottingham Forest.

Pete Sturgess – Current Head of Foundation Phase for the English FA.

Richard Dobson – Current Assistant Manager at Wycombe Wanderers.

Ryan Maye – Current Head of Coaching at Aston Villa. Coached at Chelsea, Rangers, West Brom and the FA before taking up a role at Aston Villa.

Steve Heighway –Liverpool FC Legend. Ex Liverpool Player and Ex Academy Director.

Vicky Jepson – Current Manager at Liverpool FC Ladies.

Introduction - What is Gold Dust About?

Please Note

So those reading can follow the story fluently, besides "Where Does Gold Dust Start? – By Keith Mayer" in the introduction, this book is written by David Mayer. There will be stories referring to Keith during this book.

When people feel better, they generally perform better. This book shares some of the foundations, skills, techniques, and behaviours that will help you connect with your athlete at a deeper level. There are different strategies on how you get there, but for your athlete to feel at ease with you, you have to build a connection with them. Building that connection first is important before you push for the athlete to come on board with what you're doing. The first thing successful people are good at is connecting with others, and then developing that relationship into something special.

The book is aimed at looking how you sprinkle some gold dust and verbal vitamins on your athletes' lives. Whether you're working with five-year-olds, or professional athletes, ask yourself, how can you evoke feelings that make your athletes feel good about themselves?

A lot of the foundations, skills, techniques and behaviours within the book have derived from Neuro Linguistic-Programming, co-created by Dr. Richard Bandler in the 1970's. NLP is the method of influencing the experiences people have via their senses, the communication through which those experiences are given meaning, and how people organise and programme those ideas and actions to achieve specific results. Dr Bandler is a consultant to many Fortune 500 Companies, the US Military, US Intelligent Agencies, and numerous high-profile athletes and sporting organisations, including Major League Baseball teams, NFL players and Olympic Athletes.

The examples and stories from the coaches within the book have come from our observations and their feedback over many years of coaching in their sport.

If you take at least one thing from this book that helps you become an even more highly effective coach, it has done its job. Be careful about going around trying to 'fix' your athletes. Your job is to help guide and nurture your athletes. The information in this book will only be useful if you take it to your own environment and apply it.

Where Did Gold Dust Start? – by Keith Mayer

While my son was in America eight years ago, he sent me a quote by Maya Angelou, who passed away a few years ago. The quote goes "I've learned that people may forget what you said, people may forget what you did, but people will never forget how you made them feel."

To this day, that quote has had such a profound impact on me, and it is something that has been shared with many other people in my life. It plays such an integral role in how I coach. It's such a powerful quote because it reminded me of times where I'd forget what somebody said or did, but I'd never forget how they made me feel.

I use that quote in the way I operate because I have an urge to want to help ath-

> I know if the athlete is having a positive experience, they will feel better about what it is they're doing and could also have a greater chance of learning more during those times.

letes have a positive experience. It's not always possible for athletes to have a positive experience every time they do something, but it's at the front of my mind. I know if the athlete is having a positive experience, they will feel better about what it is they're doing and could also have a greater chance of learning more during those times.

What is a Coach?

As a highly effective coach it is important to be on a constant path of growth. To grow those around you, you need to continually grow yourself.

There is a valuable lesson in where the word coach derived from. In the 15th century along the Little Hungarian Plains of northwest Hungary sat a village by the name of Kocs. In the 15th century, the village of Kocs made its living from building carts and transporting goods between Vienna and Budapest. Around this time, a carriage maker in Kocs created a larger, more comfortable carriage than any known at the time. This carriage got called the kocsi and became a valuable asset to transport goods between the Austria and Hungary.

Over the next century the kocsi became popular and was copied throughout Europe. The name became kutsche in German, coche in French, and coach in English.

> **As a coach, it is important to remember that when you are dealing with athletes you are transporting valuable cargo from one place along their path to another place.**

The word coach derives from the ability to transport goods from one place to another. As a coach, it is important to remember that when you are dealing with athletes you are transporting valuable cargo from one place along their path to another place. If we can get people there quicker, how do we get them there quicker? What is it we're not doing at the moment that we should be doing? When you change the way you look at things, what you look at changes.

You have the great responsibility to help people along their life path, so how you do that could have a great impact on their journey. There is more than one way to do it, and it is important to bring your own character on the journey.

Can you be the coach who constantly looks for never-ending improvement in yourself and your athlete? Educate yourself by watching, reading and spending time with role models and care passionately for your athlete.

Let your athlete surprise you and challenge them to become the best they can become. This requires great courage on behalf of the coach. This coach experiments, explores and has a deep passion to set high standards for themselves, their peers and their athletes.

Enjoy Your Journey

John Stevenson, Director of Kung Fu Panda, along with many other movies did a great interview in animationxpress.com. John's interview, which refers to directing a movie can relate back to most things you do in life.

If you love what you do, talk about it with a genuine passion. Your peers and your athletes will feel your passion, and in turn it can help excite them. If you talk about coaching dispassionately, you cannot expect those around you to be enthused.

> "As a coach you've got to love what you're doing. It doesn't mean it will be plain sailing, but you have to enjoy the journey."
> – Justin Holbrook.

John Stevenson believes there never really is a finished script and they are always writing and rewriting. Coaching is the same. There is no such thing as the finished script. You are constantly learning, unlearning and relearning to find out what fits best.

Involve the team around you and be open from the start. John Stevenson also believes directing a film is like being a music conductor, not the star soloist. It's very similar in coaching. Your

If you love what you do, talk about it with a genuine passion.

"It's very easy during the making of a movie for one to succumb to so many pressures, and there are all sorts of things you can focus on and forget about why you wanted to make your film in the first place. Go back to why you wanted to make your film in the first place and stay true to it."
– John Stevenson, Director of Kung Fu Panda.

job is to ensure your athletes 'in your orchestra' are playing to their best, and to empower those athletes to come up with solutions on their own.

Sir Simon Rattle, principal conductor in the Berlin Philharmonic between 2002 to 2018 has some incredible footage online on how to build connection by layering information to his orchestra. He starts by working with individuals within his orchestra, then brings it together to create a masterpiece.

Chapter 1 - The Lone Wolf: The Story of a Boy – An experience from Keith Mayer

For the purpose of the story we will call this athlete John to make it easier to follow.

Wolves are known as pack animals that live, hunt, and defend together to ensure maximum opportunity of flourishing in their environment. Similar to humans, the wolf spends the majority of their time in a group where they are stronger than by themselves. In your coaching environment you are likely to find packs within your group, but have you ever come across the lone player?

A lone wolf is an animal or person that acts independently, spending time alone instead of with a group. In the animal kingdom, the lone wolf may be stronger, and far more resourceful than the average wolf that is a member of a pack. They go under the radar because they tend to travel alone and are often looked at differently than the rest.

After 35 years of coaching, Keith came across a lone wolf like never before. It was only during this experience he started to realise what coaching really was. This experience gave him a greater empathy, understanding, and overall ability to work with athletes across many spectrums. Keith had an athlete within a group that he metaphorically called the lone wolf. The one that didn't speak to anybody, including coaches and teammates. The one who didn't look you in the eye. The one who intrigued and inspired Keith more than most.

For Keith, this was an athlete he had to work with. He had amounted all of this experience throughout his coaching and professional career and he wanted to help this athlete. John would go under the radar but would give everything he had when playing football. There was something about this athlete that was different.

Keith set off on my journey to develop this athlete in what proved to be the most fruitful experience he had ever had.

John came in as a trialist. He was a big tall athletic boy but technically required a lot work. There was something about this boy that appealed to Keith. When you asked him a question, you'd get a really simple answer, if any answer at all. You wouldn't get any real interaction with the boy, but Keith couldn't delve too deep at first because he had over 20 players that all required looking after.

At the end of the first week of his trial we signed John on. Keith understood that through to around December it was a settling in period for John. It's important as coaches that we allow athletes the opportunity to integrate with their peer groups. That in itself is a process, and even though we, as coaches, allow them time to settle in, it's important to observe how the interactions are within the group. John was still extremely quiet around his peers and the coaches. You had to really dig deep to get any interaction with this player, but it was something Keith was willing to do.

In December of that year, Keith decided to find out more about John through his Mum. Keith wanted to connect with John and his family to get some depth and understanding around what was going on in his life outside of football that may help him when he comes to practice. Over a couple of conversations with John's Mum, Keith found out there were five children in the family, all living just with their Mum, with John being the youngest. To Keith's surprise, he was also a twin. When Keith started to talk to the Mum about John and how he was very quiet, she told him John's twin sister did most of the talking for John, both in and out of school. At that point a lightbulb switched on. Keith needed to work with this boy differently. How did he connect with John now knowing what he knew?

During the conversation with his Mum, Keith asked if he could speak to John to see how his Christmas had been. The Mum shouted upstairs to get John down. When he got on the phone, Keith asked how his Christmas had been, expecting a quick and basic answer.

"It was fine, thank you. How was your Christmas?'" That set Keith back. He had a moment because that was the first time John had shown any real interaction outside of people asking him questions. Face to face he was very quiet, and people got very little from him, but Keith had one phone call with the boy and the conversation seemed different. Maybe Keith could use this platform to get more from this boy where you aren't physically in his presence.

Even with 35 years of coaching experience up to that point, that conversation was the most impactful one Keith had ever had with an athlete. Keith has worked with players that have represented their countries, and World Champion athletes, yet he was on the phone with nine-year-old boy thinking he was helping the boy when in reality, it was far from it. John taught Keith something on that phone call. After speaking with John, Keith asked John to put his Mum back on the phone so he could share what he and John had spoken about. It's important to let parents know what has been discussed on the phone so that everybody involved is aware of what has taken place.

That was the start of a project Keith called the 'Lone Wolf'. How could Keith help John further, or did he even need the help? You will come across athletes that don't say a great deal on or off the pitch. Do they have to be noisy, or are

You will come across athletes that don't say a great deal on or off the pitch. Do they have to be noisy, or are they the type of people that may be registering much more information in silence? I guess the magic may lie in the silence between the notes.

they the type of people that may be registering much more information in silence? I guess the magic may lie in the silence between the notes.

This boy had a lot to learn, but he wasn't signed on because of his technical proficiency. That was something Keith could work with. John was signed on because of his attitude. He wanted to learn. His actions spoke more than his words. Was it Keith's place to get in his world and change him from being a quiet boy into somebody who had to speak because he was too quiet? That was a big lesson for Keith. His job was to make the environment as comfortable as possible for John without changing his World, which is what he then aimed to do.

Where Keith coaches, they organise team events a couple of times a year. The age group below John's had a trip to a place called Airborne, a place where there are trampolines and climbing frames. Keith knew John had built a good relationship with another young boy in the age group below, so it was set up where John would go with his friend in the year below and see how it worked. After the event, Keith briefly spoke to John to find out how his experience was, but instead of forcing him to talk, Keith asked John if he could write what he enjoyed about Airborne and share it with Keith at their next training session. John agreed.

As promised, John brought the paper in the next time Keith saw him at training. To this day, Keith still has the handwritten paper. John wrote the following, "I enjoyed jumping and climbing on the obstacles. It was really fun when we were bouncing on the trampoline. We did some tricks and we were running around for the warmup. I enjoyed the trampoline the most because we were doing flips and we were bouncing around."

In that note, the thing Keith picked up was John used the word 'we' a lot. Keith didn't know whether that was John's understanding of the English language, or whether his interest was in more than just himself. Instead of saying what he enjoyed, was it about more than just him?

Not too long after Airborne, John and his age group had a tournament. The room lists were already sorted before the players arrive. Keith selected the rooms carefully for all of the players. It was important for him that John wasn't in a room with somebody that was going to overpower him and force themselves on him. Keith also asked John if he could write down the room list and who was staying in what room. Within five minutes John slipped under Keith's door a piece of paper with every single person's room in our party. Keith was giving John responsibility, which he took seriously.

At certain periods of the season, away trips where a regular occurrence and Keith wanted to occupy time by providing different experiences for this group of boys. On one of the trips, Keith decided they would have interviews where the boys sat down and got interviewed by their peers so they could get to know each other even more. There were some confident young boys in the group, which is a quality Keith also admires. Even though the whole experience was very informal, Keith had to ensure the questions were worded correctly and there wasn't any silly behaviour within the group. If Keith was to ask who wants to go first, he would pretty much know who it would be, but it was interesting as he went down the list. Keith believed John would want to be the last one to go, being the Lone Wolf. He was the fifth out of fourteen who stepped up.

Keith's specific question to each player that got up was "if you were not to become a professional soccer player, what job would you like to do next?" Keith wrote the answers down on flip chart paper. When John got up and asked this question, he said "I'd like to become a lawyer." As he said it, there was a moment of surprise for Keith, but he wanted to know more, so he asked why John wanted to become a lawyer. John's reply was "I want to help people." Keith asked why John wanted to help people and his response was "I want to help people who don't have a lot of money." Wow. Keith had to hold back some tears when John said that because it was an unexpected reply. This boy came from a very humble background. He lived with his Mum and four other siblings and wanted to become a lawyer so he could help people who don't come from money. The meaning behind his words were so powerful. He doesn't speak much, but he chooses his words very carefully when he does speak. For a lot of people, the power of silence can be a challenge. For John, the World he lives in is the World that works best for him.

> **For a lot of people, the power of silence can be a challenge. For John, the World he lives in is the World that works best for him.**

This is the type of boy John is. If there were balls, bibs and cones on the other side of the pitch, he wouldn't just get one. He would get everything so the pitch looked nice and tidy, and he would do it as quickly as possible. There was an experience during training when Keith purposefully left a few cones out about 50 yards away from the group when they were finished. Keith asked for a volunteer to go and collect the cones. As soon as Keith asked, John started running. Keith started to count down from 10. John was sprinting at full pace to get these cones in. As the countdown continued, the group of boys started counting too. John made it back within the countdown, and as he did the group of boys went absolutely ballistic. They were jumping and celebrating as if John had scored a goal. Up to that point it was one of the only moments where Keith had seen this boy smile. It was touching to see his peers embrace him so strongly that it created a smile on his face. His peer group that he plays with absolutely adore him. He doesn't say much to them, but they care for him.

To this day, John has no idea how much influence he has had on Keith's life and the way he now delivers and coaches. All Keith wanted to do was help John become a strong pillar of society. John doesn't have to be loud and boisterous, but could Keith help him become confident in different situations?

Keith learned so much from this experience. He needed to develop a greater understanding of the person as opposed to the athlete. The experience got Keith to reflect and ask questions about himself, which has in turn helped him become more aware of the sensitivity surrounding athletes. You may have had people ask the question, what animal would you be? If you were to ask Keith what animal he would be, he is a lone wolf. He is away from the pack, and so was John. The lone wolf, the one that acts independently, spending time alone instead of with a group. Just because somebody may be silent does not mean they don't possess big action. Just because somebody may be silent does not mean we have to invade their world and tell them they need to speak and be louder. By no means am I saying we don't want to develop them, but we need to be more sensitive as coaches to this. Do we have to force athletes to do something they aren't comfortable with? What can we do to help the athlete, rather than force issues?

> Just because somebody may be silent does not mean we have to invade their world and tell them they need to speak and be louder. By no means am I saying we don't want to develop them, but we need to be more sensitive as coaches to this. Do we have to force athletes to do something they aren't comfortable with? What can we do to help the athlete, rather than force issues?

As a more sensitive coach, Keith now works with athletes in a different way. There are many moments where he is consciously trying to help, but what he has learned is how important it is to be aware of people and their situation. If you don't know what's happening in their World, be careful about jumping to conclusions around what they need. How somebody acts currently is based around what happened in past experiences. Keith is not a social worker, but he is here to help develop athletes to become even better. He is curious around what he does, and how he can take his athletes on a journey before he passes them on to someone else.

When you look at music, you could have twenty people all playing the guitar with the same teacher and they'll all end up being different types of guitar players. They won't sound the same because they'll bring their own personality and character. We need to treat athletes in a similar manner.

It's important to remember that no one athlete is exactly the same. Steve Heighway, Liverpool FC legend is a strong believer of this. "When I'm working with athletes it isn't about me making them do something exactly how I want it to be," said Steve. "What I want is for my athletes to do something the way that works best for them. No one athlete is the same as the next. When you look at music, you could have twenty people all playing the guitar with the same teacher and they'll all end up being different types of guitar players. They won't sound the same because they'll bring their own personality and character. We need to treat athletes in a similar manner."

As long as you have the intent to influence with integrity and with a positive manner, it will brush off on other people. We want to create strong people. We're creating memories for our athletes that they can take on their journey. It is a never-ending search in the pursuit of excellence, which has and continues to keep us going.

Listen Purely, Explore Deeply

Buckminster Fuller - "What is my job on the planet? What is it that needs doing, that I know something about, that probably won't happen unless I take responsibility for it?"

Consider the notion that you cannot not communicate. What signals do you transmit in your verbal and non-verbal language that ultimately influence what type of communication you receive in return? If your intent is to deliver more effective information to your athletes, you must be aware of what's happening outside of your own World. If you pay close attention to the messages people provide, both verbally and non-verbally, you are more likely to understand the World around you, because that's where the answers lie. Opening up your eyes and ears and truly listening and watching more intently to what's happening around you. The purpose of this book is to give you more insight and greater possibility to influence with integrity and effectiveness.

John led Keith to develop an even deeper curiosity around what it is we as coaches do, and how we can develop better relationships with our athletes quicker and more efficiently. What can we do to become even more highly effective coaches? What steps do exemplars take to connect with athletes and how can we model those exemplars?

> **If your intent is to deliver more effective information to your athletes, you must be aware of what's happening outside of your own World. If you pay close attention to the messages people provide, both verbally and non-verbally, you are more likely to understand the World around you, because that's where the answers lie.**

What is the first thing you can do to build rapport with your athlete? How can you build a stronger connection with your athlete? How can you get the most out of your athletes? How can you become a more highly effective coach, quicker?

Chapter 2 - Building a Connection

As a coach, there will be processes you go through when you first meet your athlete around how you build the start of your connection. It may be something you've never thought of before. If you have, great! If not, why not? Remember, it has an impact on how the relationship with your athlete starts. This chapter looks at ways in which you can further enhance the initial connection.

Know Yourself First

"Only by knowing yourself can you be an effective leader." - Vince Lombardi

Before you want to enter somebody else's World, it is vital to know yourself, and to know your personal values and beliefs. You need to know what your purpose is. What do you believe in, and what are your values?

Beliefs are concepts or assumptions about us and the World around us. Beliefs are what we hold to be true, whilst values are manifestations of our beliefs, geared specifically to what's important to us in life.

What we identify with are the things we recognise as important to ourselves. This kind of meaning has the emotional power to shape behaviour. When you have a clear idea of your beliefs and values you will have a better understanding of yourself.

Ryan Maye, Head of Coaching at Aston Villa has strong beliefs around what is important to him when first meeting an athlete. "Before I first meet a player, I need to know within myself what is in it for me. Only then can I get an understanding of what is in it for them," he said.

"Why are they here, and why am I here? Everybody has a rationale and a reason for why they are doing something. Every player may have a different rationale and reason why they are there, but the first part is understanding what is in it for me."

Those thoughts were also echoed by Gareth Holmes, current Professional Phase Lead Coach at Nottingham Forest. "I have to understand myself first. Can I connect with that person? If not, why not?" he said. "Difference isn't a problem, failing to understand those differences is. I

Don't listen to the story, listen for the story.

think over the years you become better at relating to different people if you want to. We tend to steer towards the person that's from our area or is from the same background as us because we feel comfortable with those people. Over the years of working with different people I've got a better understanding of diversity, or what is within a person. Not necessarily where they go and where they're from, but actually a better understanding of the person and who they are."

This goes beyond sports. How many times have you found yourself in dialogue with a person but either forgot their name, or don't remember a word of what they're saying? You may look like you're listening, when in reality you aren't listening to the content. That extra bit of attention you pay could give you a snippet of information to give you a better insight about somebody. Don't listen to the story, listen for the story. If you're listening to the story you may miss it. If you listen for the story, you're more likely to pick it up. If you're tuned in to people, you'll listen for the story and you'll have a better insight of what is being said.

Building Rapport

Rapport is the harmonious relation or connection to another self. To be in rapport is to be in alignment with another person. Can you recall a time when you and another person were in harmony with

You're generally attracted to people who are similar to you, or whom you want to be like.

each other? What was it like? The chances are you felt the same about something. People can fall into rapport very quickly with people who are like them. Think about your peer group, and the people you associate with. You're generally attracted to people who are similar to you, or whom you want to be like. Neurologically, we respond more congruently to people who are similar to us as opposed to those who are not.

It is proven that if you fail to build rapport with people their conscious mind is more likely to critically analyse you as a person, rather than your content and what you can offer. When you connect with people, their unconscious mind will less critically analyse you, and will be more receptive to what you have to offer. That doesn't necessarily mean they will always agree with you, but having a receptive athlete certainly helps.

It's important to remember that whatever you do, you're dealing with human beings. You may not always get it right, but it's important that you have the intention to build a connection with people

When you work hard to make people feel like they belong you will begin to notice they will be more receptive to what you are sharing with them.

around you. When you work hard to make people feel like they belong you will begin to notice they will be more receptive to what you are sharing with them. That may mean relearning your communication strategies so that you can relate to those around you so you can see the World from a perspective that fits them.

When you first meet someone, you will be doing something that builds an initial connection with them, whether it be positive or otherwise. There will be a process behind building a connection with your athlete, but the question is, what do you want to represent to them? If you fail to build rapport with your athlete, all that is left is your point of view, and how that is viewed by your athlete. Perhaps if you consider paying more conscious attention in the direction of non-verbal signals transmitted towards us, I wonder whether your relationships could be more effective, more efficient and therefore more conducive for learning?

To be in complete congruence with a person you generally have agreement visually (pictures and images), auditorily (sounds and tones) and kinaesthetically (touch and feelings). These three main representational systems, along with olfactory and gustatory are result of the experiences you have on this planet.

Pace Before You Lead

Pacing is when you enter another person's model of the world on their terms. To pace is when you aim to match the language, experience, beliefs and values of a person to gain and maintain rapport with them.

Once you have paced a person and demonstrated that you understand where they are coming from you are more likely to be able to lead them. Leading is using the influence you have built up from pacing. If you want to lead and positively influence an athlete, it is important to know where they are now. Only then can you move towards where you want to lead them.

When you do first meet an athlete, it is possible to gain rapport quickly by pacing then leading. You are connecting and bonding with somebody to get congruence.

There will be things you may already be doing that you are not yet aware of that help you build rapport with people, but there will also be things you are not yet aware of that will help you build rapport even quicker and easier.

While pacing is not necessarily enough to ensure leading, without it the chance of success may be reduced. Finding agreement is a good way of pacing the person.

Have you ever tried to lead an athlete, or group of athletes before you have built any sort of rapport with them? When you try to lead a person or group before they feel congruence, you will notice it can make your job much more difficult.

Pacing can be done in numerous ways:

Mirroring: This will be copying what the other person does, echoing their body language and other non-verbal communication, and including sounds and voice tone.

- Examples of mirroring could be a subtle scratch of your head when they scratch their head, smiling when they smile, or talking fast when they talk fast. Mirroring works only if done subtly. If you have an athlete in your environment for the first time and you shake their hand and they smile, if you smile with them it can instantly help build the relationship.

Matching: This will be similar to mirroring, but in much less obvious ways. If an athlete scratches their head, you could scratch your arm.

Paraphrasing: This will be repeating back what the other person has said, but in your own words. You can paraphrase to test your understanding of what has been said. When you paraphrase back what somebody has said to you, it demonstrates that you have listened to what has been said.

- An example of this would be asking an athlete what they have done in school today. When they answer, "I have had English, Math and Science." You could say back, "So you've had English, Math and Science. Which lesson do you like the most?"

Parroting: This will be repeating what the other person has said to you. It is advised to only repeat short phrases. If you repeat what somebody says then pause, it can encourage the other person to talk more.

- An example of this would be asking an athlete who their favourite athlete is. When they answer, "I like LeBron James," you would say back "You like LeBron James?" and pause. You want the athlete to expand on their answer.

Agreeing: This will be simply when you agree with somebody to show you have compliance, whether you have a reason or not.
An example of this would be asking an athlete who their favourite team or athlete is and why, and then agreeing with the reasons behind their answer. If they say, "I like Lionel Messi because I think he's the best dribbler in the World," and you agree with their reasoning you have instant compliance.

Similarity: This is when you have similarities with the person you are talking to. As mentioned, you're generally attracted to people who are similar to you, or whom you want to be like.

- An example of this would be knowing people within similar circles. Like most sporting communities, the martial arts community is quite small, and people may have mutual connections. Kevin Harper is a former 2x World Champion Thai Boxer and ex High School Teacher who now owns his own nationally renowned combat gym. Since 2008, Kevin has trained over 50 Champions of all levels, including World Champions. When somebody is involved in the combat sport and goes to his gym for the first time from another gym, they'll likely know somebody in his gym. People find out a lot about him through other fighters, especially fighters recommending his gym. For Kevin, he uses that as a way to build a relationship with somebody. They have a similarity because they know the same people, and he uses that to his advantage.

Possess A Genuine Warmth

"We shall never know all the good that a simple smile can do." – Mother Teresa

Possessing a warmth makes people see you as being more approachable, caring, empathetic and welcoming. It's more likely to enable people to feel comfortable and at ease. It is difficult to fake warmth, and it can backfire if your warmth indicates that of a door to door salesman trying to close a deal.

There are still people that are big on shaking hands, and that's ok if it works for you, but we're dealing with a new generation of athletes now. It could be something as simple as a fist pump, or a high five.

Athletes are normally coming into your environment. Just as you would when people come over to your house for the first time, make your athlete feel comfortable when they first arrive in your environment.

Some sort of interaction and investment in the athlete from the start. As time passes, coaches may deem these interactions unimportant, but it's important to remember this interaction isn't necessarily for the coach. These simple interactions are an opportunity for you to show a continued interest in your athlete and vice versa.

Athletes are normally coming into your environment. Just as you would when people come over to your house for the first time, make your athlete feel comfortable when they first arrive in your environment.

Ask questions of your athlete. Show a genuine interest when you first meet them. Make it informal. Where are they from? What do they love to do? What do they love about the sport they participate in? What is their favourite sporting team? Remember, the questions are great, but the magic lies in listening to the response.

Put a warmth in your voice. It conveys emotion not only through the words you speak, but also the tone and pitch you use. Communicate with a softer, richer tone, and remember to smile. If a person is frowning or scowling, your opinion of them can be massively different than if a person is smiling. It is important to remember that when you meet your athlete, your facial expressions can have a big impact on the initial connection you build with them.

Current research shows us that smiling is contagious. It can lift our mood, as well as the mood of those around us. Each time you smile, you release neuropeptides that allow neurons to communicate. Feel-good neurotransmitters – dopamine, endorphins and serotonin – are all released when you produce a smile.

In Dale Carnegie's book, 'How to Win Friends and Influence People,' the second of his six principles is using a smile to look more accommodating. For you, as a coach, you want to influence your athletes with integrity, and you want to be able to do that as quickly as possible.

A prime example of an exemplar with incredible ability to connect with people the first time he meets them is former Premier League manager, Darren Moore. Keith first met Darren face to face whilst presenting on the South Korean Pro License in November 2017. The South Koreans came over to England for the last block of the course. Keith presented on the Pro License with Dick Bate for three years but presented to the South Koreans with Dick for over a decade. Right after their last trip to South Korea in July 2017, Dick fell ill, so he asked

Keith to organise the course with a colleague, Gary Phillips, a highly respected sports scientist.

Keith and Gary had to build a course that was structured to fit the last block of the South Korean Pro License. It involved building and putting content together, and planning club visits so the candidates could observe and listen to top coaches within England. Due to their connections within football, they were able to arrange club visits to top clubs. One of those clubs was West Brom.

Prior to the visit, Keith and Gary had never met Darren Moore. They had exchanged email and a phone calls to organise the visit, but that was it.

The Pro License cohort arrived at West Brom on the morning of November 28th, 2017. The first team had a game that night against Newcastle United, which was Alan Pardew's first game in charge of West Brom so there was a lot going on at the club that day. As the group settled in, a figure came bounding over towards Keith. "Keith, Darren Moore. It's great to meet you." From that moment, Darren couldn't do enough for Keith, Gary and the group of South Korean coaches. He played the host role. People were in his environment, and he catered to them to make sure they were comfortable.

I had heard numerous stories about how warm and welcoming Darren Moore was. When I finally got to meet him, it felt like I had known him for a long time, and I don't think I'm alone with that. He possessed an incredible warmth, and welcoming, and expressive with his language. His big frame walked across the car park and approached me with a big smile. He looked me straight in the eyes and said "David, great to meet you." Within the first two minutes of meeting him, he said my name three times within sentences. Why did he do it? He wanted to give me a sense of connection. He knew me, or at least I felt like he did. I felt comfortable in his presence.

As we sat down, we asked Darren what the first thing was he did to build a connection with people. "I want to show them I care. I ask them questions and make it about them. I want direct contact with the person," he said. "Every player I have come across is treated the same, from the first team players all the way down to the academy players. There is no extra exertion on first team players. All of the people I come across are human beings. The same consistency I had with the youth team, I had with the first team, and that consistency I used then I still use today with players, staff and any people outside of football I comes across on a daily basis."

"When I was the U18's coach at West Brom I would inter-act with the first team players just like I would with the youth team players. Every Monday I and Romelu Lukaku, who was on loan from Chelsea as a 19-year-old, would go into the canteen and analyse his performance. I have a genuine care for the people and players I work with. When you treat people respectfully, you are more likely get good responses from them."

Use the Athlete's Name

A person's name is one of the greatest connections to their own identity and individuality. It is an easy way to get someone's atten-tion, and it known as a sign of courtesy and a way of recognising that person. When someone remembers your name after meeting you, you will likely feel more respected. It makes a positive impression on you. On the flip side, when somebody does not remember your name, espe-cially if you've repeated it a few times, it can make you feel like that person is not interested or listening to you.

One thing that stood out with the several exemplars in the sporting field was their use of the athlete's name. It's something may not be thought about much by the sender of the message, but have you have you ever thought about the importance of using someone's name, or when you use it? The use of a person's name can help build an instant connection if you use their name correctly.

If I remember your name quickly, and use it to refer to you, you're more likely to feel an association to me. Now, the interesting part is how do you say the name, and where you say it in a sentence? "Tommy, great to meet you," has a different message than "Great to meet you, Tommy." The emphasis is on their name. As you will remember growing up, your parents or teachers would use a certain tone when saying your name if you were in trouble. The tone you use has great power when saying a person's name. When building the connection, if you use a warm tone it has more positive influence than if you are using a sharp and direct tone.

In May 2017, Justin Holbrook was appointed St. Helens RLFC Head Coach, leaving his role at the time as Assistant Coach at Sydney Roosters. From being asked about his interest in the St. Helens job to starting his new role in England took less than two weeks, so it was a quick turnaround. Justin was aware of the task at hand, so before he arrived, he got hold of previous St Helens game footage. Justin wanted to get an understanding of what was and was not working, and what he could change quickly. A real important thing for him was getting to know the players. Knowing how they played and knowing who they were as people.

He arrived at Manchester airport at midday on the Thursday from Australia and went straight to the training ground to meet the staff that afternoon. The next morning Justin met the players, and the day after was Magic Weekend where all teams play at the same venue over the course of the weekend.

On arrival, Justin was clear the most important thing was to call every player by their first name to show them he knew them already, and who they were. "I walked around and had a chat with every player. I referred to every player by their first name when I met them. It was important to me that there was a connection and affiliation between myself and every player in the squad," said Justin. "After I spoke to individuals, we had a team meeting. I wanted to make it clear what a great opportunity I had to coach this group,

"It was important to me that there was a connection and affiliation between myself and every player in the squad." - Justin Holbrook

and also made it clear I left one of the top clubs in the NRL come and coach them. I wasn't a coach sitting at home out of work, or at a struggling club. For me it was important the players knew I came for the challenge, and I was excited to get going."

Justin wanted to make it clear that he was excited to be there. He felt collectively as a group the players and coaches may have been frustrated, especially for a big and proud club like St Helens that were struggling. He wanted to take the pressure off the players and turn things around.

From his point of view, the players were trying too hard. The players were changing things most weeks to try and find a way to win the games and appeared a bit lost. The staff may have started to over-coach and do long video sessions and he wanted to strip it right back and simplify everything.

"I arrived on the Thursday, and our first game was on the Saturday. I gave the players and the team a couple of simple clear and concise cues for the very first game at Magic Weekend. The team went out and beat a really strong side 45-0 that game."

Justin was very clear that not for a second was he saying he had a magic formula, and to this day he still doesn't think that, but it gave himself and his staff a lot of hope moving forward for the rest of that year. It turned out to be the case. Before his arrival the team were really struggling, but under Holbrook the team showed drastic improvements from the get-go and ended up making it to the play-off semi-finals against a much-fancied Castleford Tigers team, getting narrowly beat by an extra time drop goal.

I experienced a similar experience with Pete Sturgess, the Head of Foundation Phase for the FA, who is excellent at connecting with younger children. Pete delivered on a course in Manchester to seven and eight-year-old children he had never met. He was like the pied piper. The children danced to his tune. What the attendees of that course didn't see was Pete went out early and learned every player's name by the time the session started. "I think if you talk about relationships and connecting, if somebody uses your name there is an immediate connection between you. There is so much power in me using your name than just referring to you as 'another person'," said Pete.

Do Your Homework

It isn't always possible because of your situation, but if you can, do your homework. Can you find out about your athlete before you first meet them?

At that event in Manchester, Pete Sturgess did his homework before the session. Not only did he learn the athlete's names before the session, but he also observed the players. He knew if they were left footed or right footed, he knew which child ignored everybody else and just wanted to shoot at goal, he looked at the child who wanted to go in goal. He built up a basic picture of some of their behaviours to get an insight of what their attitudes and dispositions might be like so it could help him in his session.

Mick Beale also believes doing your homework when possible puts you in a stronger position to build the initial connection. If you're in a position where it is possible, do your homework on an athlete before you meet them. In professional environments, tap into the scout or person that brought the athlete in. What excited them about that athlete? That can give you an opening of what to look out for and it gives you an opening to start a conversation with the athlete when they first walk through the front door. In professional settings it's easier because you have more access to research. With younger athletes it's important to stay close to the people that are recommending the athlete to find stuff out about them.

"I'm massive on doing homework," said Mick Beale. "If you don't have access to that, then it starts with your first conversation with the athlete. What do you love to do? Be authentic and emphasise with your voice and use your voice. A wink, a smile, a nod, a thumbs up are all massive things to kids as references that you're building something with them."

Chapter Task

1. The next time you meet an athlete for the first time, pace before you lead them.

2. Possess a genuine warmth and use their name.

3. Find out something about the athlete outside of the sport.

Chapter 3 - Building on the Connection

After the initial connection has been built, how can you grow your relationship to a deeper level? As you may be aware, it takes more than one encounter to form a solid connection with your athlete. As the coach, you will have your standards, values and beliefs that you want your athletes to abide by which is a process. To get the long term buy in that you want from your athlete you have to delve deeper and maintain the level of care you show to them.

Most athletes want to know 3 things:
1. Do you care for me?
2. Can you help me?
3. Can I trust you?

As easy as it can be to build a connection, it is even easier to lose it. If you don't have people enjoying their experiences, you'll not build a relationship with any child or adult.

If you don't water a plant, it withers and dies over time. To keep relationships alive, it is important to drop in and revisit what made the relationship form in the first place. To build on our relationships with athletes even more, we may need to delve deeper.

Gareth Holmes has five words that he endeavours to achieve within every session he delivers. To care, to serve, to inspire, to drive and to unite. When we talk about a connection, whether they're 8, or whether they're 18, or whether they're 28, the important thing is the athletes have to know that you care. This isn't about you; this is about them. You want to serve them, whether that is service in terms of putting yourself out to know them and understand them. What is their background? What are their relationships with their parents? Who are the key stakeholders in their lives? What are their ambitions for the future? What are their strengths and weaknesses? You're serving with them with a desire to know them?

Once you know the athlete you can really start to inspire them. You have a feeling for where they currently are, where they've been and where they want to go. That's their journey. Sometimes to inspire people, you have to know where they've been, and where they are now because there will be times people don't even realise what's possible. That's part of the job of a coach. To stretch peoples thinking. To nurture hope. To nurture a dream within that person, which is an incredible privilege because it means there is trust. The athlete has to know you're caring for them. You want to do the best for them. At times, that dream may seem far away for the athlete, but this is when you, as the coach, can help them on the way to their destination. You want to inspire them and stretch their thinking. You want to extend their hopes to allow them to maybe exceed their ambitions. Sometimes athletes already know where they want to go, but they may need guiding to that place. They may know the end goal but not fully understand the steps on the way to that goal. As a coach, you have to plan and understand where that person needs to go.

What is Coaching?

Is coaching about when you're structured and involved in practice? Is it about when you're in a classroom and you're doing a presentation? Or is it about the time you spend with athletes outside of that? For Richard Dobson, some of his biggest influences on a player who is now in the Wycombe Wanderers first team was when he used to take him back to his house when he was a youth team player. The player would sit in the passenger seat in the minibus, and they had 10 to 15 minutes together.

Is that coaching? Just because you aren't on the grass within the environment of the training ground does not mean you aren't coaching. If there is an opportunity to help someone or give them some information or praise you take it.

You're connecting at a level beyond the environment to help those players feel even more empowered and enriched about the experience they're having. Richard said to his chairman last year the club have punched above their weight financially, and he said there are two types of currency in sports.

> "You don't clock in at 8am and become a coach. You're always a coach."
> – Richard Dobson

Athletes can feel like commodities within sports. At Wycombe they regularly have players who come into their environment and tell them they've never had people want to connect on the level the club do. The players would tell them they didn't know where they stood with previous managers because one day the manager would have their arm around the player, and the day the manager is shouting at them. The security within the environment enables players to feel like they belong to

> "There is financial currency, and human currency. People are quick to talk about the financial side, and the budgets, but what isn't seen is the currency of human connection."
> – Richard Dobson

something special. "The strength in our club is not financial currency. It is in human connection currency". They may be poor in monetary terms, but they're hugely rich in human connection terms, and that's what makes a difference within their club.

The Journey

A coach transports people from one place to another. A journey is the act of traveling from one place to another. As a coach, your job is to positively and carefully transport your athletes from one place to another, but can you travel with your athletes on their journey?

Arsene Wenger, one of the Premier League's most successful managers ever, spoke about loving people he can go on a journey with. As a coach, even if you only work directly with somebody for a year, that is still a journey. You have the opportunity within that period, and even after that period to go on a journey with an athlete. When I reflect on the best coaches I had, they were the ones who made the effort to influence my journey even after they had stopped working directly with me.

Mick Beale said "The single biggest reason why I coach and why I'm invested in people is because the journey of where I can take people excites me. I'm there to support young people on their journey and I love the idea of helping people on their journey. When Mason Mount scored his first Premier League goal for Chelsea at the start of the 2019/20 season, I was living that dream with him. That means so much to me." Social media is not a nice place for the most part. Mick only uses social media to send messages to people about how we can make coaching better, and to send messages to players he has worked with or he likes and want to promote. Dropping somebody a little note on Twitter could help them on their journey.

What can you do to travel with your athlete on their journey?

Understand the Level of the Relationship

In life, when you listen and talk to people you are building up an awareness of where they are and how much you can impart at any time in that relationship. As conversations grow and the variety of topics get broader, the level of trust grows, and with that level of trust comes a sentiment behind the level of information you're sharing with someone.

As a coach, you're gauging the level you can impart at to impact the relationship. It might be a word, it might be a smile, or a frown. It might be something so that person knows where you're at.

Be aware of what you're asking for from your athletes in return. There has been a view that eye contact when talking is essential. Eye contact can be a bit of a prehistoric view on things now, especially with the shift in cultures. The environments coaches work in are diverse now, so to ask everybody to give you eye contact can be a mistake.

> **As conversations grow and the variety of topics get broader, the level of trust grows, and with that level of trust comes a sentiment behind the level of information you're sharing with someone.**

It's the level of relationship on a professional level. It is a caring level that the person absolutely fundamentally feels safe and cared for by you. You can only truly communicate on a level that is determined by the trust. Whether it is a 9-year-old or a professional athlete that you're talking to, it's the level of trust that will determine the level of the communication. As a coach that is what you need to seek. To build up the trust and to build up the bond.

It is important to know who you are so you can build up that trust better. You know where you are starting from so you can help the person. If you don't know where you're starting from, you don't know what your beliefs and values are, what your strengths and weaknesses are and how can you guide a person and build a trust because there is going to be an inconsistency with what you say, what you do and how you are with that player. That breaks the trust down because that inconsistency is gone.

That is on and off the field. In football you may have told the right back to get forward and overlap, but the first time he does so you then tell him he shouldn't have overlapped, he should have narrowed off. There is then a doubt in that players mind around the inconsistency within your messages.

Alignment

When everything lines up with your messages, there are no contradictions to cause disagreement. When a person receives communication from you, one way they assess whether they will trust your message or not is to compare it with other things you have said and done. If these things align, people will be more likely to trust you. However, the more your messages do not align, the less likely it is somebody will trust you.

The opposite of aligned communication is a mixed message, where beliefs, values, attitudes and prior words and actions do not line up with what is being told. If you display actions that indicate you have a history of being selfish or unreliable, then your future messages may have little to no impact.

A friend of mine who plays football at the International level told me a couple of stories about a coach who is very contradictory in the messages delivered. His team had been struggling. The messages from the coach differed, and even though culture was talked about it was apparent it became every player for themselves. The group, both players and staff had consistently been told they would not be criticized for making a mistake.

During the season a player made a mistake, costing the team a goal. The team lost 2-1. After the game, the manager heavily criticized the player in front of the media and shipped him out on loan two days later without explanation. Although the pressure in top level sports is increased and mistakes can cost dearly, was this beneficial to the player and group? When you say one thing and do the opposite, what happens to the dynamic of the group? If you want to get the best out of your group you likely need them to trust your messages, and for there to be a congruence. When they do not, they probably will not be playing for you.

Weeks after this player was criticized heavily, the club had a meeting where the Manager, Technical Director and other big powers within the club got the players together for a crisis meeting. There were two sentences within close proximity of each other that again showed a complete lack of alignment in messages from the coach.

"Nobody in this room has to worry about your jobs because you're safe, and we want you to know that." Within a couple of minutes, the same person said, "We are bringing new players in though, so if you don't perform, we will get rid of you." The mixed message again caused a lack of alignment, and I know the group of players did not trust, nor believe what was being said.

The group were completely untrusting of the manager and did not want to play for him. In these situations, it would likely be better to tell the group they would be criticized for making messages so when it happened at least there was alignment within the messages.

Darren Moore talked about being consistent with people, and having the person knowing how to act in your environment that will enable you to build that connection further. He believes your man management is so important. The best coaches have to have the ability to manage and to be adaptable. There are people who have been in the game for so long because of their adaptability, Roy Hodgson being one of them Darren has worked with. Being able to adapt your style to enable yourself to work with the different trends of people and footballers that have come through is a massive key.

> "If I'm constantly Jekyll and Hyde, my athletes won't know where to stand with me, so therefore they won't feel as comfortable with me. They may then not invest as much energy into building those relationships with me, so therefore it will take longer to build the relationship, if I can build it at all." – Ryan Maye.

If you want to build trust with somebody, you have to be genuine, you have to be honest and you have to be consistent with your behaviours, and when you're consistent, people become more comfortable with you.

Harmony

Harmony is the lack of tension. A feeling of comfort and integration. It is about fairness and balance. Rapport is about building a harmonious, empathetic, or sympathetic relation or connection to another person. Harmony is an ancient principle, used in soft martial arts that means moving with another person. When you move with the other person, it means you can move them to where you want them to be.

As mentioned, we like and trust people who we believe are like us, and who like us. When you trust somebody, you are more easily persuaded by that person.

To be in harmony does not mean you must agree with some-body at all costs or being passive but providing people with a sense that even though they do not have to agree with everything you say, there is a feeling of comfort in the relationship. If I do not trust you, then I will likely not be persuaded by what you say. If, however you appear trustworthy, then I will listen. When you harmonize with me then I feel you are like me and hence are trustworthy and that your arguments are worth considering.

Even if you tell your athlete you will listen to their opin-ions, what they tell you will be based around how harmonious your relationship is with them. When you build up a harmonious rela-tionship with your athlete where there is a feeling of comfort and integration and they are more likely to share their thoughts with you. If you tell your athlete they can tell you anything, but you have not connected at a deeper level they are less likely to want to share information with you.

Having harmony and creating an environment where the staff and players have an openness with you is important. You might be your own hindrance by ignoring the ability to listen to people. If some-body is dealing with a personal issue, that is something you may need to know because they may need support from you.

Darren Moore aims to grow the harmony within his groups. The connections built within his environment result in the transpar-ency and openness to share information. When you take the time to be aware of a situation, you may have to adapt to dealing with it, but at least you can look at a situation from a different perspective. *"Create an environment where the staff and players have an open-ness with you."*

Darren spoke about creating an environment where the peo-ple within it feel open and can share information. "In sports, you're a team, and within that team you want a strong culture with a hard-working environment, but there is also the environment where if one of us is hurting we are all hurting. That is the kind of environment I want to create on a consistent level," he said. "How many places have missed out on certain opportunities and they're wondering what happened. If they took time to get a better understanding of their person, they give themselves a better chance to address situations. How can you do that if people aren't willing to share information with you?"

What you do with the information then comes down to alignment. If you tell your athlete they can tell you 'anything' and they do, if you berate them your message is not aligned, and the trust becomes lost. The same goes when they tell you something and you care about their message. Your messages are aligned, the harmony in your relationship will likely continue to flourish.

Behavioural Changes

A key indicator of whether you've gotten through to an athlete, or group of athletes' will be when you see a change in behaviour in something you've been trying to affect. It's not as much the smile, or the high five when people are walking through the door. It's the change in behaviour that you are trying to make an impact on. Changes in behaviour are unlikely to happen unless you are consistent in your messages and hold your athletes accountable to the messages you are sending.

Athletes are very clever. You've got to be bright enough to know that they may be very clever in working you, making you think you've got through to them. The change in behaviour is a real key indicator.

For myself, when coaching, I'm a big believer on leaving places as clean as, if not cleaner than you found them. When athletes bring bottles when they arrive, all of the bottles leave with the athletes at the end of the session. When first working with a group, there is a possibility they may not have been held certain standards before and it is important to remember that. If you are just barking out orders, you may be less likely to get through to people, but if you give them a reason behind why they are doing it, and also give your athletes roles within your environment it increases your success rate.

When I recently started working with a group there were consistent reminders that bottles needed picking up after a session. It felt like a chore for me having to remind these athletes for what I perceived to be something so simple. No athlete within the group left the fields until every bottle, whether they were ours or not, were picked up.

After a couple of weeks, it was really refreshing to see these athletes were cleaning the area up without any reminder. For me, cleaning up the bottles and the area we had worked in wasn't about sports. It was about setting good standards and being respectful to the people and the environment around you. I want to help create better people, so being consistent and persistent in my messages creates a behavioural change within my athletes.

Ask Good Questions

When you ask questions, the answer you receive is generally based on the quality of the question in the first place. If the question is not provoking the response you want, you may be required to change the way you're asking your question. If you're getting short answers,

When you begin to understand the power of asking quality questions, you will notice you receive better responses.

perhaps you could phrase your question better. When you begin to understand the power of asking quality questions, you will notice you receive better responses.

One way to effectively ask better questions is to frame the question in a positive manner. Framing questions positively can help steer the direction of the conversation and leave your athlete with a more pleasant memory of the exchange. Can you ask good questions to get somebody in a great state? Instead of asking "What did you think of…?" you could say "How much did you enjoy…?"

As coaches, when we ask better questions, we are more likely to get better responses with valuable information. To further build your connection with your athletes and increase your impact as a coach, become the master at listening to the responses. The magic may lie in those responses. Listen for the story in the responses.

As coaches, when we ask better questions, we are more likely to get better responses with valuable information.

"Ask good questions then listen intently. Develop a situational awareness about people. The skill of coaching is to listen," – Ryan Maye

The Influencer Relationships

Across all age groups it is important to be parent or guardian friendly. That is not to say you become best friends with the influencers of your athlete but having a relationship with the influencer can provide insights and information on your athlete. By building a relationship with the influencer, it can help grow the relationship you have with your athlete.

On top of you having relationships with their family, you can use the athlete's relationships with their closest influencers to build a deeper connection. It's a nice touch to find out how their family is. The personal questions are important. If you want to give your expertise and influence the player, you have a better chance if you have a better relationship with them and their family.

The personal questions around influencers can go a long way. Something as simple as knowing your athlete has a sister in the Navy called Kathryn and asking how she is doing, or a dog called Billy, or Jack, and asking how the dog is. A small touch, but an indication that you have listened and have a sense of what is important to that person.

You may also face issues with parents or guardians, but as a coach your job is not to tell other people how to raise their children. Your job is to help steer them in the right path to give their children the best possible experience as an athlete. As a parent, the most important thing in their life is their children, and they want the best for their children. It is essential to remember that when dealing with parents.

There is no getting away from the fact there will be some difficult parents, but a lot of those difficult parents are only difficult because they have just been previously mismanaged. If you combine the lack of a parent's understanding for situations and the mismanagement of parents, the outcomes could be catastrophic.

The best coaches tend to have little to no issues with parents and influencers because they have clear and concise boundaries from the start, but they also deal with any issues effectively should one ever arise. Use the athlete's best interest to steer a parent's thinking to fit what you are doing.

Make Them Feel Good

If you can provide little differences that make your athlete feel good about themselves, you're more likely to build a stronger connection, whether it's something you say, or something you do.

As an example, if you find out when every athlete's birthday is and wish them a happy birthday, think of the positive feelings it can evoke. It doesn't take long to do it, but the meaning behind the message can go far. With kids, if you wish them a happy birthday it also can help build your connection with their parent. You could call the parent to wish their child a happy birthday on the phone or send a birthday card to the athlete. The difference it can make is great.

If you can provide little differences that make your athlete feel good about themselves, you're more likely to build a stronger connection, whether it's something you say, or something you do.

As a player John Terry won everything domestically at a top-level club in England. After his playing career was over, John Terry became the Assistant Coach at Aston Villa. He said to Mick Beale, "I want to be the best coach I can possibly be. I want the players to walk off the field feeling a million dollars." That's nothing to do with coaching the sport. That's about making people feel good. It's based how you are as a person and how you communicate with those around you.

Chapter Task
1. Think of an athlete you work with that you want to positively influence.
2. See this athlete and explore ways you can evoke a positive response to help further build the connection.
3. Check for any changes in behaviour, whether that is during their performance, or off the field.
4. Repeat or alter your steps based on your reflections and the changes in behaviour.

Chapter 4 - Gaining and Maintaining Motivation

"If you change the way you think about something, it changes the way you feel. Therefore, it changes what you can do, and it changes what you will do which is the most important thing to keep in mind now." – Dr. Richard Bandler

To gain and maintain motivation with your athletes it is vitally important to ensure you are curious and caring to maximise your role as the coach.

When we look at motivation, it's important to remember what motivates one athlete may not motivate the next athlete.

Building rapport, being approachable and being credible, for the most part, are the main aspects when it comes to motivating both individuals and teams. Credibility is the quality to be convincing or believable, but that does not just happen. To be credible to your athletes, it's important to have integrity and honesty in what you do, good intentions, and the capability to back up what you're saying. Once you have that, your understanding of the hardwiring of the brain for towards and "away from" motivation will help you get better results.

What is Motivation?

Motivation is very personal. In order to be motivated, most people need a precise plan or goal in mind. If you have a goal that you get really excited about there is more chance you will find the energy and motivation to strive for the goal. You're more likely to get a sense of achievement every step closer you get to your goal, and if you're motivated, you'll more than likely be flexible around changing and adapting in order to achieve your goal.

Most people do not need help doing things that are pleasant. The key to motivating your athletes is to be able to easily and effortlessly get them to do things that may have previously been unpleasant to them.

Intrinsic and Extrinsic Motivation

Intrinsic motivation involves doing something because it is personally rewarding to that person, whereas extrinsic motivation involves doing something because the person wants to earn a reward. Many coaches and parents' resort to extrinsic motivation as rewards for their athletes, whether that is offering candy, buying new shoes or boots, or giving money.

As a coach, if you find what intrinsically motivates an athlete it can

> **When you learn what internally rewards your athlete, you can use this to affect their behaviour to achieving success, rather than giving them external rewards.**

add great value. If the athlete loves beating an opponent, or scoring a goal, you can utilise that. When you learn what internally rewards your athlete, you can use this to affect their behaviour to achieving success, rather than giving them external rewards.

"Towards" and "Away From" Motivation

In life, people either move "towards" or "away from" something to get where they want to be. In simple terms, people that move "towards" are motivated by moving to what they want. People that move "away from" are motivated by moving "away from" what they don't want. As the coach, it is important to understand what helps motivate the athlete get to where they want to be. As people, all of us are governed by "towards" and away motivation, but people are naturally prone to one over the other depending on the context and situation. Your athlete might be more "towards" or more "away from" oriented, but it is highly unlikely they will ever be totally 100% "towards" or 100% "away from." The simple reason, we would be dead if that was the case. 100% "towards" would mean no fear of losing or dying. 100% "away from" would mean no motivation even to get out of bed in the morning.

Understanding the Athletes Motivations

As the coach, observing what your athlete does and listening to what they say will give you a good indication. If you ask the right questions and you are attentive and understand the language used by your athletes, motivating them becomes much easier.

> **As the coach, observing what your athlete does and listening to what they say will give you a good indication. If you ask the right questions and you are attentive and understand the language used by your athletes, motivating them becomes much easier.**

If you want to find out your athletes motivation, questions like 'why do you play this sport?' or 'what are you aiming to achieve?' may help you get a better understanding.

Cautious people are mostly "away from" motivated and may use language along the lines 'I'm not sure', 'maybe', 'it's risky' and so on. The people who take chances, risks or try out new stuff are mostly the "towards" ones. Those people will usually use language like 'I choose to', 'I want to', 'let's do it'.

A general example of "towards" motivation would be the student in school that was motivated by being the highest achiever in the class. An example of "away from" motivation would be the student that is motivated by not failing.

Here is an example in sporting context. You have an athlete that doesn't want to lose their place on the team. If you give the athlete the information they require and tell them what they need to do to not lose their place on the team, they are more likely to be motivated. You have another athlete that wants to become the best player in the age group. If you give the athlete the information they require and tell them that is what they need to do the help them become the best player in the age group, they are more likely to be motivated by that.

Dependent on the sport, and the context within the sport, it may demand certain characters within your group. If you're in a position where you are recruiting your athletes, understanding what type of character you want will help. Do you want the go-getter who may be more averse to taking risks, or do you want the more cautious athlete who may be more risk averse in their approach?

An Individual's Expectations

The Galatea effect is a theory based on an individual's expectations about themselves.   It is the belief that people's own opinions about their ability and self-worth influence their performance and is self-driven. If your athlete believes they can perform well, the chances are they will do better.

The way your athlete views their expectations about themselves are controlled by many variables, but as the coach, you have the opportunity to help guide this process. The first step to making your athlete believe they can do something is to create the strong belief they can do it. Teach your athlete to be excited when they think about their performance.

Reframing

Reframe the way your athlete views a task, and the way they perform the task will change. Reframing is seeing a current situation from a different perspective, which can be tremendously helpful in problem solving, decision making and learning. In simple terms, it means your athlete would be shifting their perspective from one thing to another to make them more empowered to act. You, as the coach, are not responsible for your athletes' experiences before

You, as the coach, are not responsible for your athletes' experiences before you met them, but your job can be to help your athlete change some of their less helpful beliefs into something more productive.

you met them, but your job can be to help your athlete change some of their less helpful beliefs into something more productive.

As an example, if your athlete says, "I'm not good with my left foot," you can reply with several different things. Here are two examples:

"Have you ever improved at something before?" or,

"What would it look like if you were good with your left foot?"

Simple replies like that will evoke a response from your athlete. You both know they've improved at something before, so to say they aren't good at something does not mean they can't get better at it. Or, by the athlete imagining themselves being good at something, it can help create a neural response to cause action. By using certain language, you can reframe situations to fit what you want to achieve.

"When you change the way you look at things, the things you look at change." – Wayne Dyer

Breaking Self-Limiting Beliefs

If you listen closely to the language people use, you will begin to notice self-limiting beliefs. If you believe you cannot do something, you will probably not do it. How many times have you heard somebody say they can't do something? If you go around and ask people if they can paint, or if they can play music there is a strong possibility quite a lot of people will say they can't. In reality, they can do it. It isn't to say they will become Picasso overnight, but Picasso also didn't become Picasso overnight. It takes time and a lot of hard work to become a master at something. If you never start you have exactly 0% of becoming a master. As soon as you start your chances of becoming a master increase.

It takes time and a lot of hard work to become a master at something. If you never start you have exactly 0% of becoming a master. As soon as you start your chances of becoming a master increase.

I had a group of players and was working on shooting with both feet. The majority of footballers are right footed, so as you can imagine, when we moved to the left side a lot of players made comments. One player in particular instead of doing what was asked, said 'I can't do that.'

It was the perfect opportunity to help break his limiting belief. His belief that he couldn't use his left foot was solely a belief. As soon as this player made the comment, I rolled a ball out and asked him to hit it with his left foot. The player made contact with the ball. It missed the goal and trickled across the by-line, but the focus wasn't on him missing the goal, or how softly he hit the ball. The focus was on breaking belief so he knew he could use his left foot. The player was congratulated on using his left foot and encouraged to do it again because now he knows he can do it. Over the course of the session this player started to use his left foot when opportunities arose. He didn't suddenly have a left foot as good as his right foot, but he was now aware that by using his left foot consistently it would improve.

That particular session I had several players who were not confident to use their left foot, but every time they did, I made a big deal out of it. I focused on the positives and the process behind the player doing something they may have previously been told they can't do, or believed they are not good at.

When you are aware of the language you use with players, you may be creating the thought that they cannot do something. How many times have you heard a coach refer to something as a weak point? When you tell an athlete what their weak foot or weak hand is, they will start to believe you. Consider what will happen when instead of referring to players using their 'weak foot' or 'weak arm,' simply referring it to 'left' and 'right.'

At Wycombe, they do off pitch development days with their players. They had a day where the whole team went to an ice cream factory, which was based around creativity and doing something new.

"Sometimes you get athlete's saying, 'I can't do that,' when it comes to football," said Richard Dobson. "We sat the players down after our visit to the ice cream factory and said 'you've been playing football for 15 years and some of you tell us you can't do something. You've never made an ice cream before, but within one day you've made an ice cream. Creativity, and being able to do something new is within you. It's about knocking the barriers down in front of you.' From a mental perspective, we want to make the players believe they can do anything."

Providing Evidence

When people are uncertain, if you can provide evidence it can be a powerful tool. The evidence can help when coming from outside spoken words. If an athlete believes they cannot do something, providing evidence that they have done something is particularly powerful for disconfirmation and destroying their belief. Providing evidence that they have done it can cause a significant emotional response.

There were players that believed they could not use their left foot in a session. Breaking the belief became even stronger when they had evidence they could and have used it. Gather evidence for your argument, and against their argument. Seek evidence that cannot be denied.

Chunking

Chunking refers to pieces of interrelated information that can be organised and expanded on. It ignites the process of exploration for chunking up to get higher meaning or chunking down for specific clarification in relation to the missing information.

No two people share the exact same reality, so each individual will chunk their information differently than the next person.

Information can be extremely detailed and specific, or extremely complicated depending on how it is chunked. It could consist of one word, a phrase, a sentence or more. By using appropriate chunks, relationships between the message will be defined. Something will never be general, specific, huge, tiny, good or bad by itself because it requires a context and a relationship to the other pieces of the chunk to define it. It's important to consider that nothing has any meaning in simple isolation.

No two people share the exact same reality, so each individual will chunk their information differently than the next person.

Chunking Up

Chunking up would be moving a specific concept towards being more general, allowing for a broader view or the ability to put things into a different context. It could be looked at as seeing the bigger picture.

To put it in a sporting context, here is an example of chunking up when working with an athlete:

Shooting > Scoring goals > Soccer > Sports > Life > Existence

Scoring goals was the original topic, chunked up to playing soccer, chunked up to playing sports, to the person's life, all the way up to existence.

Chunking Down

Chunking down would be taking a concept and becoming even more specific so the deeper understanding of the concept is explored.

To put it in a sporting context, here is an example of chunking down when working with an athlete:

Scoring goals > Shooting > Making contact with the ball

Chunking Across

As well as chunking up and down, you can chunk across to something related on the same level of what you're talking about.

If you're talking about making contact with the ball, that can be chunked across to relate to different things on the same level. Are they striking the ball with their foot on the ground, are they volleying the ball, or are they using their head? From there, you can chunk down into the more specific details of that topic.

Understanding the Importance of Chunking

Justin Holbrook is aware of the important of breaking information down to the right extent to help his players get greater understandings.

"I've found you get barriers when you're asking somebody to do something and they're not at a level to do. That is what can make an athlete uncomfortable," said Justin. "It's about making small steps.

> **Make little inroads with athletes, little steps. Adding bits to their game when they are ready for it goes a long way.**

If you're asking an athlete to do something they can't do, or haven't done, they're less likely to do it correctly, and you're likely to have issues. Make little inroads with athletes, little steps. Adding bits to their game when they are ready for it goes a long way. Therefore, when they are able to do it, they trust myself, and I trust them with what I'm asking them to do."

To motivate your athletes, you have to break information to the right levels. As Justin pointed out, if you're asking somebody to do something and they're not at a level to do, you may face resistance.

Most of us have tried to break something down to the finest details, but the athletes aren't at the level to understand it. You want to delve into great detail of tactics for an upcoming game, but the athletes only have a very basic tactical understanding. You're trying to break something down to an uncomfortable level that will likely have little impact, and if anything, could further confuse your athletes. It is important to be clear on what you're asking your athletes to do, but the athlete also has to be comfortable enough to know they can do it.

Chapter 5 - The Highly Effective Coach

There are many techniques and methods you can use to become a highly effective coach that gets the most out of yourself and your athletes. Here are some of them:

Process Over Content

Most coaches focus the majority of their time on content, and less time on the process. Highly effective coaches focus most of their energy on the process and spend less time on the content. The content is what you want to have, while the process is the way to make something happen. The process is a series of actions or steps in order to get to the end goal.

Instead of focusing on the planning and content of your sessions, focus more on the process your athletes use to learn and improve.

Every athlete has their own unique way of learning. When you can 'speak their language', it allows you to connect with them at an even deeper level. While there are many factors which influence the way your athlete learns, one of the most significant relates to which of their five senses they relate with the most. Use the learning process to find out what works and what doesn't work. There should be no such thing as failure, only feedback. All outcomes are results and opportunities to learn more.

If you notice an athlete is struggling with their decision making, at that point you may have an opportunity to intervene and help them by making life simpler. Give them more process and less outcome. You may see it with athletes that get lost in all of the tactics that go around making a team. It's important that athletes remember that you're picking them for the unique quality that they bring. Remember, your athlete is doing the best they can at this moment in time. When you give your athlete better options, they will make better choices.

The Storyteller

Humans are emotional creatures. Storytelling enables people to digest and remember information easier because it connects information to emotions. It is a fundamental human experience that unites people and helps drive stronger connections.

> **Storytelling enables people to digest and remember information easier because it connects information to emotions. It is a fundamental human experience that unites people and helps drive stronger connections.**

Influencing with integrity by using analogies and stories to take athletes on a journey. It allows them to open portals of their memories that are theirs and not someone else's. Where the athlete takes it and how that influences them induces a specific state in them. Having a clear outcome of the story you are telling can help put them in an altered state of learning.

Gareth Holmes believes a really good tool is using stories, memories or experiences that people can relate to. When he knows a person may have a really big importance and influence on a player's life, he may tell a story about a person in his life who played a really big part on his journey. Through the use of stories, you can stress the importance on other peoples' effect on that athletes life.

Storytelling can also be utilised as a powerful method for learning. Stories can help transmit knowledge and meaning. People learn from experiences through stories. I have seen coaches where they consistently use stories and analogies to get their main coaching points across. At a recent Football Association workshop, one of the tutors was delivering a session for the observing coaches. Even though the session was football related, it could fit across many sports. The session was based around the use of breaking down tight defences and attracting the opposition to then beat them. Midsession, the coach stopped the session and pulled out a large red cloth. The coach told a story about a matador and a bull fighter, then related it back to sports. The matador attracts the bull, then moves at the very last minute to evade and avoid the bull to gain an upper hand. In many sports that is what you do. You attract your opposition to expose their weakness.

There were people in attendance at the course who had seen this session before and spoke about how they remembered it clearly. The coaches use of descriptive analogies and storytelling evoke learning experiences for those present.

When you're explaining to your athletes you can make the experience more powerful by telling stories.

Anchor the Feelings

An anchor is a trigger or stimulus that retrieves a previous emotional state. On the surface, anchoring is a process similar to the technique used by Pavlov to create a link between the sound of a bell and salivation in dogs. Pavlov associated the sound of a bell with the act of giving food to his dogs and found he could eventually just ring the bell and the dogs would start salivating, even when food was not present. It was a behavioural change induced by an action.

For humans, anchors can be triggered through both environmental and behavioural stimulus. An example of an anchor is hearing a piece of music that brings back a particular emotion or feeling associated with something that you were doing. For example, when you are on holiday and hear a particular song, it creates a feeling and an emotion. At some point in the future, you may hear that song which can bring back those feelings and emotions about the experience you had on your holiday.

Anchoring is a mindset that is connected to your emotions. Everybody has anchors, and anybody can use them to evoke feelings and emotions. For you, as the coach, you can create anchors with your athletes. The way you respond to situations is an anchor. It might be a word; it might be a smile, or it may be an action.

In Western culture, it is known that a thumbs up generally means well done. When your athlete does something well, if you give an enthusiastic thumbs up to them in the height on their emotion it creates an anchor. When that athlete sees you use that enthusiastic thumbs up, it can bring back the positive emotional feeling they previously had.

Keith uses anchors artfully with his athletes. One example of an anchor he uses is 'the autograph book.' In context, when an athlete has done something magical in training, he has brought them to one side and pulled out to his imaginary autograph book for the athlete to sign. In the future, the positive feeling can be recreated by referring to 'the autograph book' with that athlete.

Be Mindful of Your Thoughts

The Pygmalion effect, or Rosenthal effect, is the phenomenon whereby one person's expectations of another person directly affects that person's performance.

In 1965, Robert Rosenthal and Lenore Jacobson conducted an experiment in a public elementary school, telling teachers that certain children could be expected to be have bigger spurts in academic growth based on the students' results on the Harvard Test of Inflected Acquisition. The test was actually nonexistent, and the children were chosen at random. Rosenthal and Jacobson hoped to determine by this experiment was the degree to which changes in teacher expectation produce changes in student achievement. Throughout the experiment, it was found that the children who were expected by the teacher to have bigger spurts in academic growth did so.

The study found people tend to perform up to the level that others expect them to perform. If you don't expect much from the people you work with, it's likely you won't inspire them to perform to the limits of their capabilities. Let them know you expect great things from them, and more often than not, you'll find that they perform better.

The Pygmalion effect explained why a lot of our relationships are a self- fulfilling prophecy. If a teacher believed a student was "gifted" or "smart," the teacher would act in ways that encouraged the student to live up to that assessment. If the teacher believed a student was "difficult" or "challenged," they wouldn't receive as much support and likely wouldn't perform as well.

The way you, as the coach, treat your athlete will more than likely influence their performance. If negative feedback is passed on to them, their performance may actually falter. Positive Pygmalion effects have a far-reaching effect on the those directly affected by it. When a coach puts faith in the abilities of their athletes, their morale and self-esteem is likely to increase, and hence, their performance gets better.

The way you, as the coach, treat your athlete will more than likely influence their performance.

Even though we could argue the study was cruel because it faltered the growth of children within the school, it shed light on the way you think about those you are influencing.

Think of a time you may have labelled an athlete 'troubled', and it so happens they become more of what you are labeling them?

It does not mean the solution is merely to say a 'troubled athlete' is now a 'great athlete' because you have said so, but in you viewing the athlete differently, your actions towards them are likely to change. Highly effective coaches choose useful beliefs that support their athletes as individuals.

"What the thinker thinks, the prover proves." – Robert Anton Wilson

Pattern Interrupts

A pattern Interrupt is an NLP technique that involves interrupting a pattern of behaviour or thoughts. It can be used to interrupt an unresourceful pattern of behaviour and can produce momentary confusion in the person.

Think of a time you have started to do something, got interrupted and then can't remember what it was you were doing in the first place.

Have you ever noticed what happens when a young player gets injured? When you notice somebody is upset and you ask if they are ok, they will generally go back into their feelings and amplify what is wrong.

Think of a time when a young athlete goes down with an injury and starts crying. When you go on and ask if they are ok, they normally cry more, and it amplifies the injury. You will start to observe that when people start crying, their eyes tend to go in one direction, and that is down to the right into their feelings.

There are a couple of ways to counteract that. One way is you can have the kid look up to you. You will begin to notice when a kid points their eyes upwards, they cannot access their feelings, and in turn will stop crying. Another way to counteract this is to break their state. If somebody is crying about a sore toe it is because they are thinking about their sore toe, but if you ask them what they had for dinner two days ago they have to access the information to find out what they ate.

The other way is by breaking the athlete's state with a harsh pattern interrupt. You may have experienced a young athlete that cries regularly. Unless they are actually injured the crying maybe seen as attention seeking. As long as you know there is no deeper lying issue, when you are coaching you may not have the time, nor do you want to spend the time with an athlete who is consistently crying. If you know the athlete is not injured, being sharper with your tone and giving them an ultimatum helps break the players state. You are shocking their system with something unexpected. All of a sudden, they aren't thinking about crying. They are thinking about your tone, and maybe a five second ultimatum you have given them to stop crying. It's important you praise them when they get up and carry on participating. If possible, include them in the session as quickly as you can, and praise them in front of everybody else around how quickly they got up.

The Art of Observation

Become a master of observation to understand your athlete needs and wants. You can't guess what is right and wrong. If you're looking for an answer, you may need to ask another question, or change the way you ask the question to elicit the response you are looking for.

"When I'm coaching, I should already know the session. Having the ability when coaching mid-session to observe the players is the fine art. Sometimes you're doing a coaching session and you think, yeah, this looks good, but are you looking at how the players are reacting to the session? How do you know the players are understanding what is going on?" – Darren Moore.

When you're coaching, if one athlete doesn't understand something, it is important to recognise if other athletes are facing similar issues. Pete Sturgess has a radar for this. He observes closely to see if anybody else is struggling to comprehend the task at hand.

"If it isn't working, I need a different approach," said Pete. "With that, sometimes I look for the athlete who does understand it and get them to explain the exercise for me. The athlete might say it in a way that helps everybody else understand too because they're of a similar age group."

You have to take it all on a situational basis, but the more experiences you gather, the better you will become at recognising what may or may not be working. As coaches, we're not always there to rescue our athletes at the first sign that something isn't going well. If we want to learn about their ability to bounce back, or their resilience we have to take them to the verge of sinking. If you've built a strong relationship with the athlete, there is more chance of them doing something because they know you're there to help if needed.

If coaches rescue too soon there are a couple of things that can happen; you don't learn how players react when things get tough, and as a coach it never gives you the opportunity to set something up where you know players may have low success rate.

Recognise when people have had low success rates, or when they've worked through something difficult, and recognise the achievement.

Pete did this with a group of athletes he recently worked with and said the following after a tough task – "This exercise was tough, but I'm watching you and when I see you keep bouncing back, I think, this player might have something special. I just love how you bounced back."

Be Aware of Mind Reading

How many times have you been in a situation where a person has presumed what somebody else is feeling or thinking, when in fact it has been incorrect information?

When you mind read you assume you know what another person is thinking or feeling without any direct evidence. Mind reading occurs when someone claims to know something without obvious evidence, claims to know how another person feels, or claims to understand another person's internal state without explanation. It is the assumptions that are made about another person's thoughts or opinions, without the other person specifying it.

I remember being told by a Dr of Psychology that if my arms were folded it meant I was close minded and was closed off to what was being said. It was something that my coach at the time picked up from this psychologist and used going forward. Whenever a player had their arms folded the coach would make point to tell them they were closed off and were not paying attention to what was being said. In reality, that was the coach presuming that was the case, and mind reading what he believed to be correct. People fold their arms for many different reasons. During a recent NLP seminar, Dr. Richard Bandler asked several people within the room why their arms where folded. The answers that came back ranged from being cold, to being comfortable, to having it as their natural position when sitting down.

Ryan Maye has also spoken about how he has sat in on CPD events with hostage negotiators that will tell you not to mind read because what you may think somebody is doing may not actually be true. If you're crossing your arms, somebody may perceive that as negative body language, when in reality you may just be comfortable. It's dependant on the context.

Before you make a negative assumption around a person's thoughts or feelings, it's important to understand why they are doing what they are doing. Your assumption around something can hinder the relationship you have with that person.

However, there will be occasions where you can use mind reading language to give your athlete the suggestion you know what they are thinking or feeling in a positive manner. If you were say to your athlete "I know you are excited to train today," you are using a mind read to indicate you are aware the athlete is excited to train. Even though that may not have been the case, you are presupposing they are excited, and the athlete may think deeper about what has been said.

> Before you make a negative assumption around a person's thoughts or feelings, it's important to understand why they are doing what they are doing. Your assumption around something can hinder the relationship you have with that person.

Situational Understanding

Until you have understanding of an athlete's situation it can be more difficult to have a lasting impact. The Lone Wolf was a story of a boy who had a different situation. Knowing that situation helped develop the connection.

Keith had another experience when he was coaching the U16's at Nottingham Forest. His team played on Sundays back then, so they practiced on Saturday mornings at 9:30am. There was a boy within that group that came from a single parent family in a tough part of Nottingham. He had never been late before, but on one particular day he wasn't at practice on time.

"I'll never forget seeing him come up the drive of the training ground," said Keith. "Normally when a player arrived late, they would get a bit of stick from the lads, but when this kid arrived nobody said a word. It wasn't until afterwards I found out this boy got three buses to get to training, and one of the buses broke down on his route to the training ground that day. This kid had to get three buses to training, and three buses home. Midweek when we trained, we were the last group to finish at the academy at 9pm. I had never given it much thought until I found this out."

Gareth Holmes also spoke of a similar experience. For Gareth, punctuality was massive. They had a 7:30am leave for game, and for Gareth, when you were late, you were late. It hit 7:30am and he shouted for the bus driver to leave. One of the coaches turned around and told Gareth one of the players wasn't on the bus. He didn't care. It was time to leave. The coach turned around and said, 'we need to wait,' and Gareth wanted to know why. As Gareth was getting the explanation on why they should wait for this player, the player comes on his push bike like a bat out of hell down the training ground road. It was only afterwards that Gareth found out this player had biked over an hour to get to the training ground at 7:30am, and he was going to say the bus had to leave because this player was a minute late. "Thereafter I was more aware of the importance of having empathy and knowing the situation of a person before you dish out consequences."

In his book, 'Leading with the Heart,' Coach K from Duke University talks about having a buddy system, so players were responsible for each other. He speaks about how lots of rules keep people

You may have rules in place, but there may be extenuating circumstances behind a person violating the rule. Understanding the situation before handing out punishments may be important, because you want to get to the heart of the problem.

from decision making, which can be built around being the dictator as the coach. Coach K, who is one of the finest College coaches of all time wanted to be a leader, which is an ongoing process of adjustment and flexibility within boundaries. You may have rules in place, but there may be extenuating circumstances behind a person violating the rule. Understanding the situation before handing out punishments may be important, because you want to get to the heart of the problem.

"The fact that I don't have a hard and fast rule gives me flexibility. It provides me the latitude to lead. It also allows me to show that I care about the kids on my team and it demonstrates that I'm trying to be fair-minded." – Coach K.

Time is important, and punctuality is important, but getting a greater understanding of the players reasons can be more important. We're very associated to our own feelings and experiences, and we have our own standards that need to be maintained. Equally, getting to understand somebody else's situation is important too.

We're very associated to our own feelings and experiences, and we have our own standards that need to be maintained. Equally, getting to understand somebody else's situation is important too.

Be Mindful of Other Interactions

It's important that coaches are sensitive around other interactions that are taking place around them. I've seen it happen many times where an interaction is taking place between a coach and an athlete, and another coach comes in and interrupts and interferes in the interaction without having any understanding of what is going on.

The coach that is interrupting may have little idea what they are doing. As a highly effective coach, be mindful and sensitive of those interactions. You may need to listen in and find out what kind of conversation is occurring in the first place. If you blindly barge into a conversation, remember it may cause the message within that conversation to be lost.

The Power of Unspoken Words

Harmony can be spoken dialogue, but it can also be physical. As mentioned, harmony is an ancient principle where you move with another person to then move them where you want them to be. Kevin Harper, twice Thai Boxing World Champion demonstrated, and talked about getting his fighters to experience harmony so they could move their opposition to where they want.

With his high-level fighters, Kevin gives up his time and works with them for free. The extra pad time not only takes his relationship further with his fighters, but he also knows it develops the fighter's abilities. He talked about experiencing moments where they do pad work and no words are spoken. As the fighter develops, they read him in a skilful way. They read his body movement.

"I'm not telling them what to do," said Kevin. "In martial arts anybody can stand there and say, 'do this, do that,' while holding pads.

What I want to do is mimic a future fight, or previous performance to a really high level. High speed, high quality."

When a fighter reads you so artfully and skilfully it becomes like a dance. One person leads, and another person follows. Kevin leads a martial arts dance and the fighter can follow it in such a way that they're able to match almost everything he is doing. There is no spoken dialogue, just a physical connection that happens. That's what he aims to recreate at the highest level. The slightest movement indicates a certain reaction, and he's looking for his fighters to observe that without any spoken dialogue. During a fight he can't tell them what is coming, but if they have mastered the art of observation, they can recognise what is coming without a spoken word taking place. It's top level stuff. You're trying to recreate accurate pictures of what could and would happen in a real life scenario in the sport. It's choreography.

The Power of Notes

For coaches, you may have encountered an athlete who does not verbally communicate. Coaches are quick to tell athletes to 'talk and communicate' because they're too quiet, without understanding why they are saying it. In reality, the player is already communicating messages to you by not verbally communicating. Have you ever investigated to find out why the player is quiet?

As we know, the Lone Wolf didn't communicate much in person, but was more receptive over the phone and went into more detail when writing messages down. Can you use the power of writing?

Not only can you utilise this with your players, but as a coach you may need to write stuff down too. For Mick Beale, he has a good memory around smaller details with his athletes, but he also writes stuff down. If somebody has a brother or sister, or a dog, he has been known to write that information down to use. Later down the line he will ask the kid how the brother or sister, or dog are doing.

The Mavericks and Master Locksmiths

In sports, you generally need an athlete with bit of magic to create something special. When you've got the maverick or master locksmith, can you include them in what is happening? After all, those types of athletes have got such a huge impact on how your side is going to perform. Justin Holbrook likes to include these types of athletes because as coaches need them to buy in, and if they buy in to how you're going to play your side is going to play better. "I enjoy including my players in what is going on," said Justin. "It's important to remember that you will have players that are your coach on the pitch for you."

For Holbrook, he's worked with some of the most elite rugby players in the World. From his personal experience, he has found these elite players tend to be a bit different, which in itself presents different challenges. The elite athletes are wired like that for a reason, and that's part of what makes them so great.

"It's important to make them aware of the impact they're having on the group, because when things don't go your way, they can to lose their marbles," said Justin. "They're asking so much from their teammates because they demand so much from themselves. These players can be the best to work with, but also the hardest to work with. Different situations trigger different outcomes, but you want those types of players around, and you do need them. Giving them a clear understanding of the team values and behaviours and letting them know how important they are is critical. With the elite players the mental side of their game is big."

A big thing Justin drives home to his players is if players want to be the best they can be, they need to be able to let things go quickly during a game. That is an area Justin worked really hard with this group around, reiterating that it's important to let the last play go.

"If I don't care about what has just happened, I don't want you to care about it," said Justin. "Having a trigger to move on can help, so even it's a simple phrase such as 'move on,' then that's fine. Athletes may have an initial disappointment with a mistake, but the best ones move on quickly to their next job. It's been a big focus for me."

Chapter Task

1. Think of an athlete or group you work with that you want to positively influence.

2. Pre-plan a scenario where you can tell a pre-planned story, anchor a positive feeling, or interrupt a pattern to evoke a positive reaction.

3. Check for changes in understanding or behaviour by asking a follow up question or observing.

Chapter 6 - The Highly Effective Communicator

The words you use, the way you say those words, and the way you carry yourself has a direct impact on those around you. As humans we rely on the way we communicate to share our experience, and to help create positive experiences for other people. Even though you may not have been aware of it previously, you often limit yourself through the language you use, but it is easy to change.

Can you imagine being consciously aware of what you're saying, when you say it, and how you say it?

> **Speak in such a way that others love to listen to you. Listen in such a way that others love to speak to you.**

The Use of Your Words

Embed Commands

People embed commands in others through language. An embedded command is an NLP technique to plant a thought within the mind of another person. Coaches that get success across the board will be good at embedding commands in their athletes. They're clear and concise in what they want, and the commands they give are understood by the athletes.

By using embedded commands, the message you send can be received subconsciously by your athlete making it easier to remember in the future. To successfully embed a command within your athletes, some of the things you require would be a well-formed command or suggestion, appropriate timing and lowering the tone of your voice while raising your volume.

"As you begin to *listen to me*, you will begin to *learn more*."

"You will notice how *good it feels* when you get success from *working hard*."

"You can *begin to relax* when you are *participating* because you *perform better*."

Embed Questions

An embedded question is a question within a statement. I'm wondering if you understand what an embedded question is?

Phrases that are commonly used to introduce embedded questions are things like:

"Do you know..."

"I wanted to know..."

"I wonder…"

"Who knows…"

"I'd like to know…"

"Would you mind explaining…"

"I'm curious to find out whether you..."

Instead of directing a question at a group or individual, you can subtly embed a question.

"Can you do this task?" becomes "I wonder if you can do this task today."

The Use of If

People use the word 'if' without understanding the disadvantages it may bring. The word 'if' implies that something may or may not happen and dilutes your influence with the possibility of failure within your athlete. You can use other words just as easily to consolidate your influence. Read these following examples:

"If you don't learn to use this pass, you won't be able to unlock more doors during the game."

"If you use this type of pass, you may be able to unlock more doors during the game."

"When you use this type of pass, it will enable you to unlock even more doors during the game."

The first sentence has implied it likely won't happen with unhelpful language being used. The word 'if' in both the first and second sentence has implied the athlete may or may not master the pass, whereas the word 'when' has implied the athlete will master the pass. A simple word change has presupposed something is going to happen to the athlete.

"Before you get this turn right, try it one more time..."

"While you are here you can enjoy learning during our training session."

"When you continue to work hard you will notice how much more success you get."

The Use of But

Think back to a time when somebody said something complimentary to you, but then paused and added a 'but.'

"I love you, but you need to clean up your mess." What happens in your mind when the person says the word but? As humans, our emotional response is to ignore what went before the but and to focus on what came after it.

The word but has the potential to negate or cancel what goes before it. It is generally accepted as a signal that the important part of a sentence will follow it. When you use those words, most people listening will give more attention and more weight to what you say after the 'but.' As a coach you can evoke unwelcome responses with the wrong use of the word. The words 'however' and 'yet' can be used in a similar way. "Well done today, how-ever."

It is possible that the person speaking intends on being helpful or complimentary. Using one of these words can take away the effect they are attempting to create.

There is, however, a good way to use these words as long as you're aware how to use them. If you want to acknowledge some-thing negative but emphasise the positive alternative, the word can have a more powerful outcome. The two sentences below are very similar, yet very different in the effect they have on the receiver of the message.

"You did some good stuff today during the game, but you need to im-prove your passing."

"You can improve aspects of your passing, but you did some good stuff today during the game, and you should be happy with your performance."

"We've had a lot of chances on goal, but it is still 0-0 at half time."

"It may be 0-0 at half time, but we've had a lot of chances on goal. If we continue to move the ball quickly, we will put ourselves in more opportunities to score."

Darren Moore used a great example of this while at West Brom. The team were going through a spell where teams were putting 10 men behind the ball against them.

He said to his team after a game "We've drawn the game but give yourself a pat on the back because teams are coming here and don't want to come and play. That now gives us an opportunity to work on something on Monday, as a group we will explore ways to unlock teams that defend with 10 men behind the ball."

I wonder if you can think of a time you have said the word "but" and it may have evoked a negative response. How could you change that situation if a similar situation were to arise again? You may have not used it correctly last time, but I know you will learn from that and use your words better next time.

Instead of using but, you could also replace it with other potential words. For example, you could replace the word 'but' with 'and,' or 'even though.'

"You played well today, but you know you can improve."

"You played well today, and you know you can improve even more."

The Benefit of Providing Options

Giving your athletes options can help give them a sense of empowerment without you losing control of the group.

This can work effectively because it can be a win-win situation for you as the coach. You're only offering choices that are okay with you. The athletes can pick one that fits them better so they're happy, too. Continually forcing something on athletes can go astray if they don't want to do something, so giving them a sense of autonomy within your boundaries can be useful.

"Do you want to do this now, or in 10 minutes?"

This is known as a double bind choice. It presupposes the action you want your athletes to take. You're just giving your athlete a choice as to when.

The Power of Agreement

When a person acknowledges that a number of things are true, they are very likely to believe the next you say is valid, whether it is true or not.

Ask your athletes several questions where the answer is easy to answer and is 'yes'. After you've asked several questions that have evoked a 'yes', ask the question at the end where you really want the answer 'yes'.

For added agreement, use your own body language to get agreement. Encourage your athletes to say yes by nodding your head gently as you talk with them.

"Do you enjoy playing games?" – "Yes"

"Great. I'm guessing you enjoy scoring goals too?" – "Yes"

"Fantastic. It's a good feeling scoring a goal, isn't it?" – "Yes"

"If you enjoy scoring goals, it's important to work hard in that area, isn't it?" – "Yes"

Ask Questions to Get Permission

When you ask your athlete's specifically tailored questions it can also give you their permission to work with them. Presupposing you have something that will benefit the athlete can help get their attention.

"If I had some information that could help you become an even better athlete, would you be interested in finding out what that may be?"

"Are you interested in learning something that will help you become even better than you already are?"

When your athlete understands how they improve, they are more likely to strive towards the improvement. The brain is a muscle, so the more it is exercised, the stronger it becomes. Every time they try hard and learn something new, their brain forms new connections that, over time, make them better at what it is they are practicing. Understanding that growth is within the athlete's hands. Knowing how they achieve the growth is an important tool to have.

When your athlete understands how they improve, they are more likely to strive towards the improvement. The brain is a muscle, so the more it is exercised, the stronger it becomes.

Athletes often see practice as a place where they perform for the coach to judge them. The growth mind-set changes the perspective for your athlete and makes your practice a place where the athlete is engaged in developing for their own benefit. As a highly effective coach, you will help your athlete gain the tools they need by keeping them focused on the process of achievement, which include hard work, continual effort and willingness to take on new challenges.

Speak to Individuals Within a Group

You can make a statement, tell a story, or ask questions that can have a direct effect on specific individual so they feel like they are being spoken to personally, even though they may be part of a larger group and you haven't mentioned their name.

It is important to be artfully vague on purpose.

"As you work through today's practice,"
"I know you have learned something recently."
"I don't know what you have learned today, but I do know if you continue to work hard it will benefit you"

The key in the message is you are artfully vague, but you have targeted a specific person, or people within the group. To take it another level, you can use your body to target this person even more without ever saying their name.

You may use an artfully vague sentence and look around at each person as you are speaking, but as you are talking you can use an open palm to direct the message in their direction it can have even more power. It is a subtle message that can be picked up by the intended receiver of the message.

As you begin to tune in your senses, you will notice this person may sit or stand there and start nodding their head in acknowledgement of what you've said. The biggest indicator of success in your message is the change in behaviour afterwards.

> **The biggest indicator of success in your message is the change in behaviour afterwards.**

I had a recent experience of this with a group I had only worked with twice. I had been informed that there were some players within the group that were known for not giving the effort that is required in each session. There was one player in the group that was well known for this and it was very noticeable from the start of the session. I brought the group together and addressed the players who were known for lacking effort, in particular this one player.

"I know there are people within this group that are not working as hard as they can, and I know you know who you are. It's important to know that people are observing you so when you are working hard it is noticed. You will also begin to notice that the more effort you put in, the more success you will find." – While speaking, I directed this mes-

sage at the one player by opening my hands up and pointing them in his direction during the key parts of the sentences. For example, when I said, *"you know who you are,"* I used that moment to subtly point in the direction of this one player. The kid was nodding his head at what was being communicated.

At that point, I had an idea my message had gotten through, but it needed to be tested. The players went back out and the one kid was giving considerably more effort. When he gave effort, it was important to revisit my message and let him know I saw his effort.

"Well done, John. I saw what you did there when you worked hard to get the ball back." The positive reinforcement emphasises my original message that people are observing the hard work and it does get noticed. It gives the player a reason to work hard again. He knows I know when he is working hard, and he has been told his effort has caused his team to get the ball back.

Steve Heighway also had a great example of being artfully vague with an older group he was coaching. After a specific session, Steve said to the players, "there are four or five players in this group that have shown massive improvements over the last six-week period. For the rest of you, don't get left behind in the rush to be a great player. I'm giving you an open invitation to catch up and I urge you to take it."

White Noise

Be aware of how much you speak. You may have met the coach who talks too much. Over time, their words become white noise because athletes tune out. It is important be consciously aware of how much you're talking, and also how your audience is reacting to what you are saying. If all of your athletes are asleep, it may give you a good idea you've bored them.

Justin Holbrook has a good feel for himself when he is talking. When he feels like he is speaking too much he knows it.

"It's a long season in rugby, so you need to be consciously aware of what you say, and how much you talk," said Justin. "The way I try to get around that is to empower the assistant coaches, and players within the group. My assistant has video sessions that they're responsible for, and on the field, they'll have drills they control, and I step back and observe. It's really important that your own voice doesn't become a boring one because if players become bored, they are less likely to do what it takes to be successful."

It's not enough to have good intentions. You are responsible for the impact of your communication. You can begin taking even greater responsibility for your impact by becoming very aware of your use of your words.

It's not enough to have good intentions. You are responsible for the impact of your communication. You can begin taking even greater responsibility for your impact by becoming very aware of your use of your words.

The Use of Your Voice

It's not just what you say, but also the way you say it. You could word your messages correctly and know what you want to evoke from what you say, but how you say it dictates whether the message will come across correctly.

Darren Moore is a coach who is aware of the variations in his voice. When he was at West Brom, they played in a local derby where there was no need for a full blooded, full tempered speech. The atmosphere was already there.

"When you're speaking to a group or an individual, it's important to know what you want from them. If you want them to be excited, you need to put excitement in your voice. If you want them to do things quickly, you may speak quicker. If you want them to be calm and listen more intently, you may speak slower." – Mick Beale

"I needed to be calmer, and I recognised that," said Darren. "The volume of my voice, and how fast I spoke could tip the group over the edge. The team was already charged up for the game after being out for the warmup, and in that moment, it was just a subtle reminder to play the game and not the occasion. There was a calmness in the way it was said. If I went in and started shouting and attempting to get the players going, I may have over exerted energy into the players that tips the scale too much. On the other hand, I remember we had a long journey down south for another fixture, and we arrived at the stadium where there was a nice, calm family atmosphere. As a coach, you have to be aware of details like this, because I've seen it happen where you have an away game and go into environments like this and come out flat and end up losing the game. If you settle into environments without influencing your players, you may have failed them. You have to have a level of consistency in what you're doing, but fine tune it to suit the environment and the current situation. Your athletes can very much ride off the way you use your voice, and you need to be aware of that"

As a coach, how many times have you heard yourself speak? If you don't know what you sound like, and how your voice works, how do you know you can't change or tweak your voice to get more out of it?

Ryan Maye knows when he talks quicker and louder, he sees a direct correlation with the increase in tempo and people moving faster. When he talks quieter and slows his voice down, his players listen more intently. Pitch, tonality and tempo are all conversational skills that straight away can evoke a physical response from people.

"How well do you know how your voice works? Singers know because they get instant feedback from the people listening," said Ryan Maye. "As coaches, we're saying stuff and giving information that we want responses from, but we may not have any feedback on how our voice is affecting the group. Understand how your voice works helps you interact and understand how you may be able to improve it to help get more out of those around you. I'm very aware that I have a high speed when I talk. I had no idea I spoke quickly until I first went up to Scotland at Rangers. For the first time in my life I found people couldn't understand me. I was having people telling me to slow down because I was talking too fast. If you've never listened to yourself speak, how do you know how you sound when you say certain things?"

Understand how your voice works helps you interact and understand how you may be able to improve it to help get more out of those around you.

"I know that when I raise my voice, I sound aggressive," said Ryan. "When I shout across the pitch it may sound aggressive to the players, and they may receive it in a certain way because of how I sound. If I'm not aware of that and haven't addressed it, everyone on the far side of the pitch may think I'm not happy with them. I know when I go into a new group of players, I let them know that if I shout it may sound aggressive because I know how I sound. If you feel I'm having a go at you for something, or you don't know if it was positive or negative, ask me and I can clarify it. Straight away, I'm letting the athletes know what I think I know. I'm helping the athlete's tune in to me by giving them clues and ideas around how I operate, and how things may come across when I do or say certain things."

Steve Heighway believes learning from people in different professions is a great way to recognise the importance of the use of the voice. "When you look at how doctors talk, they speak softly so you listen more intently," said Steve. "They do that for a reason. The way they speak forces you to listen. The use of your voice, and how you speak comes from experience. You won't learn that from a coaching course."

Your voice is a very flexible and extremely powerful tool. By varying the volume, pace and pitch you can alter the meaning of what you say and invoke different responses out of your athletes.

Volume

The volume of your voice can dictate how much emphasis you are putting on things you say. If you say something quietly, it can draw your audience in, but if you say something loudly it can make them pay attention, quickly.

Pace

Make sure the speed of your delivery is appropriate for the occasion and easy to follow. If you speak too quickly or slowly it can be become difficult to follow. If you want your athlete to do something quickly, try speaking quicker. Think, if you say, 'get the cones in fast,' but say it slowly, you are less likely to get the result you want. Adjust the pace to help dictate what you want to achieve.

Pitch

The pitch of your voice varies depending on the context of what you're saying. If you're asking a question, it goes up. If you're making a statement it goes down.

Experiment with the way you use your voice and begin to notice the changes in your athletes' reactions with what you say.

Breathe and Pause

The quality of your breaths affects the quality of your voice and the ability to speak clearly. You can use the pauses while breathing to great effect. Your message is not only conveyed by your words, but also by your pauses. When used correctly, it can give those around you time to absorb what you have said. If you don't use the effect of a pause, your athlete can get lost within your messages. Think about the way you use your pauses to allow your athletes to process what has been said.

Be Aware of Your Body Language

"People may hear your words, but they feel your attitude." – John C. Maxwell

People drive off how you lead them. If your job is to lead 20 people every day, there are more eyes looking at you than you are looking at them. Some coaches may not realise, but if you aren't yourself people are likely to pick it up. How you walk out before your session, or how you walk into the office is picked up. Being aware of the consistency in your approach every day is important. How you approach everyday affects how your people react to what is happening.

> "People may hear your words, but they feel your attitude."
> – John C. Maxwell

Coach Energy

Your energy introduces you before you even speak. For Justin Holbrook, the way he approaches his sessions is something he is aware of. There are times he has had training sessions and, in his words, 'he's

People drive off how you lead them. If your job is to lead 20 people every day, there are more eyes looking at you than you are looking at them.

come out and been a bit cranky.' At St. Helens they created a culture where players felt comfortable, and he's had players come over and let him know, in a nice way. People pick up on the way you approach each day things.

Justin is a big believer of coaching energy, and he's big on his staff coaching energy too. Your athletes can drive off your energy, and if you want to create an energetic environment you need to portray energy as the coach.

"I'm big on coaching energy because you have to set the standard yourself," said Justin. "If you're walking on to the pitch moping what do you expect your athletes to do? When I get out on the field, I need to set an example, so I'm upbeat, I'm lively, I'm passing a ball or kicking a ball around. I want to set the example to show how good it is to be out there. Whether it's a beautiful sunny day, or we're getting hail in the face at minus 2, I reiterate to the players how good it is for me to be out there."

"I'm big on coaching energy because you have to set the standard yourself." - Justin Holbrook

You may see and hear some coaches that believe if they put on a session and it's not working, it's the athlete's fault and not theirs. As the coach, what can you do to raise the energy within the group before it drops too far? Your energy can come through the use of your voice, how you intervene or maybe how you run around. If a group is lacking energy your whole demeanour will need change because if it doesn't and the low energy session continues, the dip may be so deep that it'll hard to get the athlete out of it.

Chapter Task

1. Think of an athlete you work with that you want to positively influence.

2. See this athlete and hear the conversations you have been having.

3. Think of a set of suggestions/commands you just wish you can get this person to respond to.

4. Generate a set of well-formed suggestions with a time frame at the end.

5. Check with the examples above to confirm your suggestions are well formed.

6. Repeat 1–6.

Chapter 7 - Effective Praise

In today's society, we're very good at telling people what they aren't good at, but we aren't particularly good at focusing on what is good and what we can improve on. Surely, as coaches we should be telling athlete's what they do well so we can get more of what we want.

A lot of coaches look at what athletes can't do and make a judgement based on that, or the level they're going to be at, then they stop watching. If we stop watching, none of these late burners, or these late developers would ever get seen. In England, Mick Beale believes we've lost a lot of soccer players we could have had because we looked at what they can't do, and we stopped watching them.

> **Surely, as coaches we should be telling athlete's what they do well so we can get more of what we want.**

Richard Dobson finished playing at a young age due to injury but learned a lot from the experiences he gained as a player which help shaped him as the coach he is today. He told a story about one of the coaches he played under as a youth footballer.

"When I gave my best and someone shouted at me for getting something wrong, that hurt me because I was giving everything I had," he said. "When I had coaches on my back when I was giving everything it used to annoy me. I used to think 'I'm giving you everything here. I don't always get it right, but why are you on my back when I'm giving everything I've got?' That was an early moment that made me realise I didn't want to be that type of coach to people that were giving me everything. I wanted to encourage effort, inspire and look at more positive words than to shout at players. My experiences as a player made me realise, I didn't want to be the coach that other coaches had been to me, and I made that decision very early on."

When an athlete makes mistakes can you look at the aspects

in which they can improve, rather than berating them for the mistake? How can you do that better next time? What can you do to keep the person balanced rather than going from fear factor, to being ok with them? It's highly unlikely an athlete makes a mistake on purpose, and the chances are they will know they've made a mistake. If you, as the coach, consistently berate mistakes, you may compile a negative feeling that will stick with your athlete.

As the Assistant Coach of Wycombe Wanderers, Richard draws from his past experiences to help create a special environment at the club.

"I'm in dialogue with the boys to let them know I recognised what they've done. I look to praise players when they do something that we've been working on. I encourage them to do the things they're good at as much as they possibly can. If you're a good dribbler, I encourage you to dribble at the right times. One big thing I ensure I do with my players is emphasize the hard work they've put in, and that's something I tell the players I have recognised."

When his players have performed and worked hard, he is quick to encourage that. Win lose or draw, he has sent a player a text if they've played well and worked hard. A little reminder after the occasion that he recognises what they're doing. The consistency in his message is evident.

When you jump from emotion to emotion players tend to not know where they stand. "For me it's about having a balanced environment and having very few changes in my demeanour on a Monday after a game whether we've won or lost," said Richard Dobson. "I look at the first team players now and I'd like to think they say it's the same me that comes in on a Monday morning regardless of the result."

Richard works hard to steer clear from the emotional rollercoaster that sports take you on, which he believes is a big thing that helps his relationships with his players. Players can see the coach's emotions, and they sometimes try and take where they think should be and how they should behave off the coach's emotions. If you're a coach who lives on an emotional rollercoaster week in, week out, the athlete will generally reflect that.

A great analogy that one of Richard's players spoke about to him about at the start of the 2019/20 season is 'it's not being a tugboat and always pulling people with you. It's being a lighthouse and guiding people.' It's a wonderful analogy for the type of coach he aspires to be.

The way you praise or berate your athlete will influence the way they feel around you, and how they may view future tasks.

There are ways in which you can guide your athlete to get more of what you want from the communication you use. It's important to remember that when you are positively precise with your communication you should get better results out of your athletes. The way you praise or berate your athlete will influence the way they feel around you, and how they may view future tasks.

Praise Effort, Especially in Children

World-renowned Stanford University psychologist Doctor Carol Dweck has done decades of research on achievement, success and the power of the human mindset, especially with children. Dweck found through her research that it's not just a person's abilities and talent that bring them success, but the way they approach the task at hand. Through her research, Dweck found that praising intelligence and ability doesn't encourage a child's self-esteem and lead to accomplishment, but actually can jeopardise future success.

With the right praise, it is possible for you to motivate your athlete and help raise their levels of competence, willingness to complete tasks, and to continue to work through challenges they may face.

Many people are under the impression that consistently praising a person's intelligence helps builds their confidence and motivation to learn, and that a person's inherent intelligence is the major driver behind their success and achievements. Dweck's research showed that the first belief is false, and the second belief can actually be harmful to a child's development.

The way praise is used with children is closely linked to how they view their ability, and generally leads them to hold one of two beliefs:

- Intelligence and ability are a fixed trait.
  - o Children with fixed mind-sets become overly concerned with how good they are at something and tend to avoid tasks that will not amplify how smart or good they are. The desire to learn and get better takes a back seat over the preference to be seen to be good at something. These children tend to care a lot about what people think about them and avoid challenges where mistakes may take place. Ability trumps hard work and effort

- Intelligence and ability can be improved.
  - o These children tend to believe they can develop how good they are at something, and they focus on doing that. As opposed to worrying about how good they appear at something, they want to take on challenges. They have a better understanding that being a master of something takes lots of work and effort. They will care and invest in learning and developing, and believe effort is a positive thing that causes growth.

Dweck's research has found how you praise people's successes has a direct impact on the mind-set they develop, especially with children.

In "The Perils and Promises of Praise" by Carol Dweck she said the following: "I think the way we praise, the way we talk to kids, all of these messages are conveying a value system. So, when we say to someone 'Oh, you're so smart', it says that's what we value. When we say to a kid 'Oh, you did that so quickly, you're really good at it', we're telling them doing something quickly and easily means they're good at it, and if they

Effectively praising effort can help drive athletes to do more of what it is they are doing to get more success.

have to work hard, they aren't good at it. Or if we say 'Wow, I'm really impressed', and they haven't really worked hard, then we're saying that's what impresses me – that if they make a mistake, if they struggle, it doesn't impress me."

As mentioned, consistently praising somebody for being smart or good at something does not increase their self-confidence and help them enjoy learning. Praising an athlete's ability will give them a short burst of well-being, but constantly using this praise is linked to the athlete in believing their ability is a fixed trait. It can make the athlete more fearful of making mistakes, less willing to work hard to improve and learn new skills, and more prone to struggle with difficult challenges they may face.

Praising for effort and applauding your athletes for the process they use can create motivation, increased effort, greater self-confidence, willingness to take on new challenges and a high level of success in future endeavors. Effectively praising effort can help drive athletes to do more of what it is they are doing to get more success.

Know Who You're Praising

For Kevin Harper, you have to praise athletes, but on different levels. Some of his fighters are looking for consistent feedback and praise, and want to know what they're doing well, whereas others are internally driven don't require as much feedback and praise. There are different levels of praise, but for him the fighter always needs to have earned the praise. In his gym, the sessions are tough and demanding. It's an environment where you are expected to work hard. The skill content is high. The fitness content is really tough. People go into his gym and go through that, and Kevin wants to acknowledge that, and let them know he's seen what they're doing.

At high levels in fighting Kevin praises the performance first because to get to a high level you have to put the effort in every day. It's expected. If you don't put in the effort you won't be competing at a high level.

The praise is different for every athlete because it is personalised to them.

Professional athletes don't get to their level without putting in effort. He wants to praise the performance, and the things the fighters did correctly to get good results.

With the children in the gym, Kevin praises effort first. He tells them he recognises the effort and applauds them for that. Remember, you want the younger athletes to know you value their effort.

The praise is different for every athlete because it is personalised to them, but it depends upon if they're competing or not. He looks to layer things. What is the next thing the fighter needs to work on to get better? 'That was excellent. You've done really well there. Now that you've done that, can you do this as well?'

Be Specific with Your Praise

Along with concentrating on your athlete's effort over anything else, in the book 'Teaching Excellence' by Richard Bandler and Kate Benson, they state the best way to maximise praise is by linking it with a specific activity. Each step tells your athlete to feel more confident as they gain more competence. Be specific in your praise and be aware of the age of your athlete. Here are a couple of examples of what effective and specific praise would sound like:

Remember that at younger ages it is proven praising effort helps build the child.

"I love the effort you put in to get yourself in that goal scoring position. The way you recognised the opportunity to work hard to get in that position showed, and that's why you got your opportunity."

"You really worked hard to get back in position then. I saw the effort you put in to get yourself back to help your teammates out. Fantastic work."

"The effort you put in today showed in your performance. It was a tough game, and sometimes things don't always go the way you planned, but the fact that you continued to work hard is what impressed me the most."

The older your athlete gets, you can impact them positively by praising their performance.

"The way you recognised your opponent's movement was fantastic.

Your ability to evade and avoid that punch showed. Keep observing your opponent's movement, and you will see your chance to strike."

"What a fantastic pass. I love how you recognised that pass early."

"What a quick learner you are. You identified when to make that wonderful pass."

"How did you learn how to use that pass? You must be a great listener"

"That was a premier league pass. How did you learn how to do that at your age?"

There may be occasions where your athlete works hard but struggles. In those situations, it is still important to gear your communication towards the effort, and at working at things your athlete can do to get even better.

"I loved the effort you put in today. This week we will work hard on your right foot so you can continue to improve."

"I loved the effort you put in today. This week we will work together and figure out what you maybe didn't understand to help you next time."

What about the athlete that may find things too easy? If you have experienced that as a coach, you will understand the importance of keeping this athlete motivated and challenged in a group setting. You want to ensure your athletes are challenged, and if they're at different levels that can become difficult.

Giving athletes individual challenges to push them is something that can help. When you do this, it is important that your athlete knows why you are doing it.

"I can see you're finding this easy, so I'm going to challenge you to help you become even better."

Consistent Mindsets

Athletes who have a growth mindset understand their abilities can be developed through hard work and dedication, which can be directly impacted by your praise. Having a fixed mindset is believing your qualities are fixed traits and cannot change. As a coach it is important to have a growth mindset about yourself and your athletes.

It is possible for somebody to have a different mindset about themselves than about other people. Can you remember a time when you came across a coach that had a strong growth mindset when it came to their own development, but a fixed mindset about their athletes? That coach may have been continually looking at ways to improve and maximise what they were doing and wanted to perfect that. When it came to athletes, the athlete may have lived in fear of going to the coach or performing in front of the coach and getting their disapproval.

An example of this could be a coach who pushes themselves to improve their own knowledge and wants to grow but berates the athlete every time they make a mistake. The mistake would be seen as a failure rather than an opportunity for learning, and the athlete can live in fear around attempting something in case they make a mistake.

The athlete may have a growth mindset about themselves, but as a coach you have the ability to steer their mindset in different directions with the language you use, and the connection you have with your athlete. The higher up you go on the ladder within sports the more pressure is involved.

Environmental Differences

When working with younger players in environments that acquire less pressure, the urgency in what you're doing is less than in a professional environment. You have much more time to work with your athletes, and you have time to help shape and mould them as people.

Your role within the environment can dictate your reactions to mistakes. As a First Team Manager, the pressure and eyes are consistently on you so the room for error is much less. The Assistant Manager will likely endure less pressure, and so on. It's important to understand that pressure situations can push the importance and urgency of what you're doing because people have to react and make judgements quicker in professional environments. There are times when you may need to be tough on mistakes, but have you worked hard to revisit your relationship with an athlete afterwards?

Darren Moore and Ryan Maye both talked about the pressures within sports, and what can be done to ensure you're revisiting the relationship with your athletes.

There are times when you may need to be tough on mistakes, but have you worked hard to revisit your relationship with an athlete afterwards?

"When you assume responsibility as the first team manager, you have to be more selfish," said Darren. "The relationship still exists and I still care for you, but the pressure means I have to act differently to do what is best for the club and for the team, and that may mean the player I care for may not play today because there is somebody else better suited for the game."

"Things can quickly unravel when you don't return to home base in the relationship. You may have a close relationship with an athlete, but the pressure of the job in a given moment may mean you have to be selfish about what is best for you and your team. If afterwards you don't revisit that relationship and allow it to wither you will become a parasite. Over time that relationship dies," said Ryan Maye.

You will have good times, bad times and indifferent times in relationships, but you have to continue to revisit the relationship and work through it.

The comparisons between a relationship and keeping a plant alive are similar. If you don't recognise a plant is dying because it needs feeding and needs watering, you may have killed it before you even realise what has happened. On the flip side, overwatering your plant can also kill it. If you're over managing a relationship it can also kill it. Constantly bouncing around scattering praise is not necessarily linked to useful learning.

> "Things can quickly unravel when you don't return to home base in the relationship. You may have a close relationship with an athlete, but the pressure of the job in a given moment may mean you have to be selfish about what is best for you and your team. If afterwards you don't revisit that relationship and allow it to wither you will become a parasite. Over time that relationship dies," said Ryan Maye.

I heard of a story of a guy who was a manager in a business who went on a leadership course to improve his relationship with his staff. When this guy got back from his course his relationships with his staff ended up dwindling, and none of his staff wanted to be around the manager. After studying the environment, it was found that the manager had been told to consistently go around praising his staff on his leadership course. His staff tuned him out and found his constant praise as fake and had no interest in what he was saying. It is important for you to understand the environment you are in, and to understand the athletes and people you are working with.

Regardless of the environment you work in, if you give clear guidelines and expectations it lays the platform, so people are aware of their boundaries. Andy Cole, ex Manchester United player once said about Alex Ferguson "everyone understood what was expected from them and were held accountable for their actions. If you lose and Sir Alex believes you gave your best, it is not a problem, but if you lose in a limp way then mind your ears." Set your expectations early and make your athletes aware of what it is you expect, and follow up on the positives, but remember, if they aren't doing what is expected, you will need to deal with that too.

> **Regardless of the environment you work in, if you give clear guidelines and expectations it lays the platform, so people are aware of their boundaries.**

Chapter 8 - The Silent Whisperer

Effective communication goes way beyond personally passing messages to your athlete. Can you be a silent whisperer? The silent whisperer is an artful way of sending messages via a third party. Use your influence as the coach to influence other people to communicate to your athletes or staff members.

Quoting someone else can increase the impact on learning, so messages passed on to another person can feel even better than being passed on first-hand. Sometimes you have to realise there is another person who is the conduit that can be used to get the message across to a person. If there is another person that may have a bigger impact or has a better relation-ship with an athlete than you have, can you let them pass information on?

> **Sometimes you have to realise there is another person who is the conduit that can be used to get the message across to a person.**

One of the greatest managers in history, Sir Alex Ferguson, eluded to bringing the right people into players' lives at the right time. Having that skill set as a coach to understand what is right at what time.

Think back to a time when somebody has passed on a message that you've done really well, and think how good and empowered it made you feel? You've been recognised outside of the environment you operate in.

How Can You Be A Silent Whisperer?

When observing your athlete, think of who else can have a positive impact on what your athlete has done. It is possible to use other coaches, staff parents and guardians, or even other athletes to pass on a message.

If your athlete who has done something well, can you take the athlete to another member of staff who saw or commented on what was good and ask that member of staff to speak to the athlete about what they'd seen? Or, can you take the athlete to another member of staff who hadn't seen what was good and have the athlete tell the coach what they had done so well? By putting athletes in front of somebody they may not know, or who may be a senior figure is an unbelievable way of an outside person giving praise to a kid at a young age that reinforces behaviour. It's off the field coaching, but it has a massive impact when you use other people. Sometimes you can be a voice that gets drowned out if you're not careful, so utilise what you have around you.

Nick Marshall, Assistant Academy Manager at Liverpool FC said "Sometimes you have to accept you won't build a trusting relationship with a player. Sometimes you have to realise there is another person that can be the conduit who can get the message across to a player. I've got no issue having another person having a better relationship with a player than I have. If we've got 150 kids under our wing, I'd be delighted if I can form a strong and significant relationships with five to ten of them. I'd much rather have a really talented group of staff that can do the rest of it. Part of it is having a lack of ego and understanding that other people can have those relationships. If it has to be you, you have to work hard, and take time to build the relationship."

Whisper to Outside Influences

Nick told us a story about an experience with ex England International, Michael Dawson when he was a 15-year-old schoolboy at Nottingham Forest. In the summer times the coaches used to bring the players in to the National Water Sports Centre in Nottingham.

"Michael probably can't even remember this," said Nick. "It was a bit old school, but if players were late, or making noise after a certain time we would go for a run in the morning around the centre. There was one night when quite a few of the players made noise after curfew, so we ran the next day and made it a race. Michael came in last. He was growing and his legs were all over the place, but I thought he was coasting as he had finished last a few times. I felt at the time I was probably a face and voice he had gotten used to. Jamie Hart, Paul Hart's son, who at the time was a professional cricketer, was with me. I mentioned to Jamie 'You're a professional athlete. Go and speak to Michael and tell him you noticed he came last, and you felt he maybe could be doing better, but also give him some of the experiences you've had on your path to be a professional athlete.' Jamie would have reinforced what I had previously said to Michael, but I wanted to show Michael that it wasn't about me, and my opinion. All of a sudden it was coming from a different perspective."

Whisper with Situational Awareness

Can you be aware of allowing people to be put in situations where you have a good idea they're going to succeed? If you put people in situations where you think they may succeed, they are in positions where it could be someone other than you that is going to give the praise. It may be peers, it may be colleagues, other athletes or the parents. Having an athlete succeed gives more possibility of receiving praise outside of yourself.

In sports we talk about athletes moving up an age group. If you feel an athlete is ready, you can move them up at the right time knowing they'll receive praise from other areas.

Gareth Holmes eluded to an example of something really simple. He had a new player in the group that was really intense and needed help settling in. Gareth knew the kit man at the club was a great with people.

"Knowing the kit man was the first-person people see in a morning, I told the kit man to spend a bit longer with that player and have a laugh with him and make him feel comfortable in a morning when he arrived at the training ground. It was bringing the right thing in at the right time."

Gareth was aware of the situation and adjusted accordingly. He utilised someone within the staff to positively affect one of his players.

Whisper to Your Inner Circle

Anybody who has met Justin Holbrook knows he talks very highly about his group of players and staff. Even in press conferences after a poor performance you will not hear him talking poorly about anybody within his circle. He praises the group, and he knows it gets back to the group. As a person, he has said he would rather praise come through him, but it is evident Justin is a silent whisperer.

You can be a silent whisperer with your athlete, but it's important to know you can do it with your staff too. If you normally present in front of your team or your athletes, but you have a really good feeling and you're really aware that a staff member can succeed and excel in that environment, then give them the responsibility to do that. You trust that person, and you know they'll get praise from other people, and your staff may also realise that you trust them in that environment, too.

Justin regularly utilises his staff to not only present, but to pass on messages. The club staff play a huge part in the team's success because Justin has created an environment where that is possible. They have presented in front of the team, in front of other staff, and also in front of individuals. If a player needs improvement in a certain area, Justin discusses it with the coach in that area who will then spend time with the player. Justin doesn't sit in on that meeting, but he will reinforce the message when he sees the player afterwards. Something as simple as "Did you go through your defensive shape with the defence coach? Great, that's what we think can help improve you becoming even better."

Not only does he utilise his staff, he also utilises and gives his players responsibility. He told a story about a player in his team he wanted to work. He used another player within the group who had a real connection with the player he wanted to work with. If you're thinking that you may not be the right person to get the message through, you could speak to a player who does have a good relationship with someone you want to work with, whether they travel to training together, or they have a strong friendship outside of sport.

"That's another reinforcement for that particular player to understand we care about them, and we're trying to help them get better," said Justin. "If a player is getting a message from the head coach, from the assistant, and from his best mate on the team it's a reinforcement of what we're trying to do. Once again, it's positive and it's constructive. It's for a reason, and this is going to make you better."

Creating Other Whisperers

At Wycombe Wanderers they've got a leadership group of four players within the squad called 'The Generals'. Rather than having one or two people, they wanted to have four people that can manage all different types of people in the dressing room. They hold the qualities and values the club want. Every month the coaches speak to 'The Generals' about the squad. They talk about who may be in a good place or who may require some assistance. They have had times where a player may have split up with their girlfriend, so as a group they've come up with a plan to help that specific player. They utilise the four generals to pass messages on. If the coaches need to get involved further down the line, they will, but the staff let the players take ownership of situations because they're closer to each other than the coaches are.

Last season Wycombe Wanderers were in relegation battle and had a couple of games where they had been the better side but got beat 1-0. After one particular game, the squad were frustrated and felt they deserved to win, so the emotional side of them caused mini arguments between players in the changing room. Richard Dobson remembers speaking up and saying "now is not the time. Cracks appear in the social structure of relegation teams, and we will not allow those cracks to appear here."

On that day when they lost 1-0, Richard calmed the situation down. After he spoke, he looked across and made direct eye contact with one of the generals within the group. The generals understood they had to play a part in diffusing this situation. One of the generals in the group then went over to speak to one of the players who was emotionally fiery at this point. He did a brilliant job speaking to the player, and totally deflected the anger.

"It doesn't always come from me directly. Sometimes it comes from mentoring other players within the group to take lead in situations. Instead of you having to confront a whole dressing room, you've got four players on your shoulder who can also help you do that very quickly," said Richard.

With the generals, the staff have also given them younger players to mentor. The younger players don't know they've got a mentor, but the generals are over their shoulder helping them out. The generals are instructed in the following way, 'in a game if you see a player work hard, tell him. If you see him attempt something and it doesn't come off, reassure him and tell him to have another go. The more you do that to players, and the young player receives praise from you, you can become a bigger influence among the group because you're seen as a real positive character.'

It's important that the players feel empowerment and are gathering the skills to become better mentors and leaders.

Vicky Jepson also utilises senior players at Liverpool to influence the younger players within the group. Today's generation are more likely to want things now much more than in previous years, and as coaches we all have to adapt to that. There are several instances where an athlete doesn't get what they want straight away, and they switch off and want to go somewhere else. They may not embrace the challenge of pushing through tough times, so your challenge as the coach could be working with the player to ensure they have the resilience to keep pushing.

At Liverpool, Vicky has used her captain to whisper messages to younger players to keep pushing. She has previously informed her captain of a specific situation and told her to let the younger player know she is happy with where she is at, but she has to keep pushing and working hard.

Whispering Through Notes

When Pete Sturgess was the Head Coach of the England futsal team, they were playing Lithuania in a qualifying game they had to win. The night before the game, Pete wrote on small pieces of paper a quote from people of influence. Every quote was personal to what each player brought to the team. Pete put all of the quotes in envelopes and gave them out. He watched their faces when they read it. Some were perplexed, but some got it straight away.

"That was a little way of me sending them a message about something special they bring to this team," said Pete. "We won the game, and it wasn't because of that, but I felt closer to the players because of what I did. I wanted to tell my players what I thought about them, and what they brought to this team."

They were all handwritten quotes that were personalised based on what the players had contributed through training, through games, both wins and losses, their willingness to go above and beyond what was expected. He wanted to recognise what these players do to go above and beyond. For Pete, he wanted his players to know they were all on the journey together, and he wanted his players to know that he appreciated them for what they did and what they brought.

Chapter Task

1. Think of an athlete you work with that you want to positively influence.

2. Explore outside influences that you can utilise to help this athlete.

3. Think of a scenario where you can use the outside influence.

4. Generate a set of well-formed messages this person can pass on to your athlete.

5. Follow up on the messages passed on with the person or athlete afterwards.

Chapter 9 - Thank Your Athlete

As coaches, we applaud what athletes do well, but how many times do we thank them for allowing us to be there to witness what they have done, thanking them for the effort they have put in, or for doing something magical?

A simple thank you to your athletes or peers has the ability to show your gratitude and appreciation towards them. It is shown that appreciating somebody makes them feel good about what they do and can help make them feel better about themselves.

During a recent season, Keith had an opportunity around a player he coached. It was instinctive, and it was an appropriate moment in context. This player, who has a wonderful left foot, picked the ball up and passed a ball out wide left to a teammate. As his teammate collected the ball to get himself in to a crossing position, the player carried his run forward. The teammate put in a lovely cross straight to this player who, on the run hit the ball on the full volley straight into the top left corner.

It was one of them moments where everyone who was observing applauded, but also couldn't really believe what they had just seen. It was a special goal, and Keith felt like he had to recognise that. After the game Keith asked the athlete who brought him because he wanted to speak to them. Only one of the players parents had brought him that day, so before they left, Keith got them together in a quieter but infor-

> As coaches, we applaud what athletes do well, but how many times do we thank them for allowing us to be there to witness what they have done, thanking them for the effort they have put in, or for doing something magical?

mal setting. He said to the player 'I want to thank you for allowing me the opportunity to witness such a special goal.' The short dialogue was meaningful and extremely useful. There Keith was, thanking a nine-year-old boy for sharing such a memorable moment. That moment was an eye opener. Parents enjoy plaudits from people who are in a position of influence on their child. The parent passed the message on to their partner, who then contacted Keith and thanked him for spending time with and helping their son. It was a meaningful dialogue with a young boy by thanking him for allowing Keith to see what he did.

Highly effective coaches want to help athletes and coaches be better and are also open and receptive to learning. Keith passed his experience on to Justin Holbrook, who has since found himself thanking his players in context now.

"What a different way of going about it," said Justin. "So many people will say 'what a goal, or what a try,' but to actually thank them for allowing you to witness what they've done, or for the effort they've put in creates something else."

During St. Helens' record breaking 2019 season, they had, at the time, their hardest game of the season. 1st vs 2nd. The game was a bone rattler in front of an electric atmosphere, which St. Helens won. The players were exhausted from that game and had to follow it up by jumping on a bus and traveling up North for a game against the team who were sitting 3rd. In blustery conditions in front of a very quiet crowd, the Saints went out and dominated from the start, going 40-0 up. After the game, Justin thanked the players for what they did. It's so easy to talk about 'knowing what to

> **"So many people will say 'what a goal, or what a try,' but to actually thank them for allowing you to witness what they've done, or for the effort they've put in creates something else."**
> **- Justin Holbrook**

do and doing what we did last week and make it happen,' but it's so hard to do. For the players to do that, he felt it was right to thank them.

On an individual level when he talks to the players, he also thanks them. He has pulled players aside and thanked them for their performance and for how hard they've worked. In sport, Justin tends not to reward the big play or the big pass, but rather he rewards the big chase, the big tackle, or the massive the effort.

Do your athletes play for you because they want to, or because they have no choice? That is something that sits deep with Justin knowing that. Are his players enjoying what they're doing? He believes it's a two-way street. He wouldn't expect his players to enjoy him if he doesn't enjoy them. Love your players. Care for them. When the players run out to perform it's important to think good things about them. If you go out with bad thoughts about your players, it can turn into bad things.

In Justin's two-and-a-half-year spell at St. Helens it was extremely noticeable what his players and staff thought about him. They cared about him, enjoyed his company and wanted to play for him.

In one of his last interviews before departing for the Gold Coast Titans in the NRL, Justin said he wanted to be remembered as somebody who 'did his best day in, day out for the players, for his staff and for the club he worked for.' He thanked his players for what they have brought to his life, and he truly meant it.

From a results perspective, Justin will go down as one of the most successful coaches in St. Helens, and Super League history with over an 80%-win rate in a two- and half-year spell after taking over a mid-table team. Results aside, Justin is one of the most revered people in the history of a rugby club that formed in 1873. He epitomises the highly effective coach that touches peoples souls and provides everlasting memories and experiences for those he comes in to contact with.

Chapter Task

1. Be aware of future scenarios where you can thank your athlete for something they have done.

2. Think of a set of commands you want to get across to your athlete.

3. Set up the situation where you can positively get this message across in the right place.

Chapter 10 - Minister of Care

"People don't care how much you know until they know how much you care." – Theodore Roosevelt

A minister is somebody that attends to the needs of someone. They act as a minister in their specific field to tend, care for and look after people. The best coaches have a greater affinity to caring for their athlete. One of the biggest ways of creating relationships with an athlete is going the extra mile. If you just turn up, do your session and leave you'll find it very difficult to build a connection with an athlete.

The minister of care is the coach that goes the extra mile to look after the well-being of their athlete. The experience the athlete has can be very dependent on the way they are treated by you, as the coach. The coach that goes the extra mile to care for their athlete will be the one that likely has the biggest impact on them. As a coach, we are creating memories every time we are with our athletes.

> **"All the best coaches I've seen go the extra mile for the athlete. They care for their athlete."**
> **– Nick Marshall**

We're building evidence, and a portfolio of information that we're gathering. There may be something within that information you've gathered that you recognise you can do something about because you care.

The following chapter shares stories and experiences from people who have gone the extra mile to care for their athlete. The stories vary from a small gesture, to something much bigger, but they all had a positive impact.

I recently met a grassroots soccer coach that personifies the minister of care. For those who don't know, grassroots soccer is amateur soccer played by young kids from the age of six through to 18. It is run by volunteers who give up their time for free to coach and work with kids to give them an experience in soccer.

This coach works as a taxi driver in Liverpool. His income is dependent on the hours he puts into his work. Despite knowing he would make more money working more hours at work, he spends multiple hours a week working with a group of inner-city kids for free and has done so for over five years now. He is at every practice and wakes up early on Saturday's and Sunday's to coach his team during games.

The coach's son plays on the team, but he has become a second father figure for many of the kids, and the main father figure to others.

He travels around the city of Liverpool with his son picking up these kids to take them to and from training and games. He feeds them, he gives them advice, and he cares for them as if they were his own kids.

Liverpool is a great city, but it also has its fair share of crime and gangs. Without this coach, some of these kids would be on the streets and may even be getting involved in crime related activities. He is going well beyond the norm to care for these kids. He isn't doing it for accolades and recognition. He is doing what he is doing because he cares about those boys as people.

I have a lot of admiration for grassroots coaches. Many of them give up their time and go above and beyond to help these kids have a positive experience.

A Little Gesture Can Go a Long Way

Nick Marshall spoke about an experience he had with one of the top players both he and Keith had worked with where a small gesture by Keith went a long way.

"I remember when one of our better players was watching a younger age group train from the side-line. Keith went over and got the player involved to do demos," said Nick. "I look at that and think how powerful that made the player feel. Keith cares for the welfare of his athletes and cares about making them feel good. That one small gesture helped that player tremendously."

Something so simple yet so effective. It epitomises being curious around what is possible when exploring different avenues. Thinking outside of the box to involve those around to empower them.

Come Dine with Me

Wherever Mick Beale has been, he has encouraged his staff to grab breakfast, lunch or dinner with his players, which led to a Gold Dust moment. Instead of doing that in the professional environment, could it be done elsewhere? Mick came up with an idea based off the TV show 'Come Dine with Me.' It became a welfare event where coaches and staff members went to the players houses and had dinner with them to see how they were living outside of football in their own setting. There were learnings with Mick and his team that he previously did not know.

Protect Your Athletes

During fights, Kevin Harper is consistently one of the first coaches in the UK to throw the towel in when his fighters start getting hurt. He's well known for throwing the towel in if his fighter isn't in a good place. He has seen fighters get really hurt and their corner won't throw the towel in.

"Particularly with kids and non-professionals, they're going to school or work tomorrow," said Kevin. "People do this for fun and enjoyment, and I don't want somebody's life outside of that fight to be affected because I wanted to keep a fight going."

"I do this job because I care. In those situations, I look at it as living to fight another day," said Kevin. "If I see a kid getting distressed the towel goes in. I look at it from a parent's perspective. I may be disappointed that my child didn't win, but I'm also very glad that the coach is looking after my child. I wouldn't let me child get a beating. I wouldn't let anything happen to anybody that I wouldn't let happen to my own child." Kevin does that with every single person that fights for him. He invests in them heavily because they're representing him, his gym, and themselves. He puts the upmost time into them. If a fighter is in trouble and they're getting hurt, they're coming out of that fight and together they will work on what they can improve on moving forward.

Care About the Wellbeing of Your Athletes

"In sports, I'm aware that only a tiny fraction of athletes will get to the top of their sport, but as coaches we should all do what we can to make sure every athlete has a wonderful experience from start to finish." – Steve Heighway

For Justin Holbrook, the reason he goes above and beyond for his players is because he is interested in them. Coaches talk about it, but it comes down to your level of interest in the person. Justin doesn't want to only talk to his athletes about rugby league from a playing perspective because they're in the team.

"I want to have conversations to find out what my players are interested in," said Justin. "That's something I use that I can relate back to. Knowing if they enjoy golf, or what movies or TV shows they've recently watched makes my day easier. I'm doing it for myself as well as building a relationship with that person. It's giving me something to talk to my players about outside of the professional sport. I can't spend all day only thinking about the sport, and I want my players to be the same."

> "In sports, I'm aware that only a tiny fraction of athletes will get to the top of their sport, but as coaches we should all do what we can to make sure every athlete has a wonderful experience from start to finish."
> – Steve Heighway

Justin know It isn't about making his players play better because he knows what shows they watch, or if they go to a driving range the day before a game.

"I need my players to play at their best, and whatever helps them do that I will do, but it's about me enjoying my job, and enjoying being around these people. I want to do it. I'm big on the wellness and wellbeing of my players. It's becoming bigger in sports, and so it should be."

Not only does Justin do what he can for his players, but he has an emotional attachment to the town of St Helens. He believes if you've got an emotional attachment to something, you will try harder.

"I try so hard because I know how much rugby league means to the people of St Helens," said Justin. "A lot of people in this town base their weekends around our result. It's a great responsibility, and one that I enjoy, but for players, if they feel the club is invested in them, they'll try harder for the club. It's a continual process. I care for the players, I care for the staff, I care for the club and I care for this town."

Mick Beale shares these thoughts and actions about caring for the wellbeing of his athletes. There are several athletes he has worked with that he has gone the extra mile with to help them. There was a boy that Mick worked with that had a bad experience previously and was released by a big club. Mick spoke to the kid's Mum and took it upon himself to help this kid out. He went above and beyond to bring him into the club he was at because he wanted to help him. He spent time in the afternoons working with and helping this player. That was going the extra mile, because it was going beyond

"I need my players to play at their best, and whatever helps them do that I will do, but it's about me enjoying my job, and enjoying being around these people. I want to do it. I'm big on the wellness and wellbeing of my players. It's becoming bigger in sports, and so it should be." - Justin Holbrook

the boy. He went directly to the people around the player that worry about him the most.

"I wanted those around the boy to know he will be alright. It's nothing to do with me being a psychologist or a therapist. It was me getting to know the boy and understanding what made him fall in love with the game, and what he enjoys about life. I got to know this kid. You have to back your athletes and support them in what they do. Sometimes they may let you down, but that happens. Go the extra mile to help your athletes."

There is a player Mick is working with currently to show him he cares. Mick is doing nothing special other than letting him know he cares about the player and he's with him, regardless of how he plays. The player can mess up, but he knows Mick is with him. When he goes out to play, Mick will put his arm around the player and encourage him to be himself, to enjoy the experience, and to know Mick is with the player whenever he crosses that white line. The athlete knows Mick is with him. That comes from the challenges he gives them, the consistency in his messages, the conversations he has with them and the amount of times he checks in with them around their welfare.

Sport is about coaching individuals. The individuals will then make the team stronger. It's the athlete's journey, it's their life and it's unique. By working with the athlete and coaching them on an individual level, you will make your team stronger.

The stuff Mick does like 'come dine with me' and taking the time out to speak to the parent about the athlete is going the extra mile. Along with that, here are a few of other examples that Mick does to show he cares. He has gone to watch a game with an athlete before they go out on loan, he has watched them train when they're on loan, he has to watched them play when they're on loan, took the time out to meet them in the off-season for a coffee and catch up, and took time out to plan a session specifically for that player. All those things are going the extra mile.

Sport is about coaching individuals. The individuals will then make the team stronger. It's the athlete's journey, it's their life and it's unique. By working with the athlete and coaching them on an individual level, you will make your team stronger. It is not about chasing athletes. You need to respect the relationship you have with them but be there to help them when they need it.

Chapter 11 - The 21st Century Coach

"Do the best you can until you know better. Then, when you know better, do better" – Maya Angelou.

How many coaches take time to reflect on their experiences and look at what the 21st Century coach will look like? Coaches want to know what the 21st Century athlete needs to look like. When you adapt and learn to become a 21st Century coach you're enhancing the opportunity to create the best athlete possible.

> "Do the best you can until you know better. Then, when you know better, do better"
> – Maya Angelou.

To be the best you can be, it is imperative to keep learning, reflecting and growing from your experiences, whether they are good, bad or otherwise.

As people, every experience we go through shapes us in one way or another. Some experiences are completely unexpected, but they will have an impact on who we are as people and as coaches. When you look at Steve Heighway's journey, from being a Liverpool FC legend as a player to founding Liverpool FC's Academy, and becoming their Academy Director, he had some experiences that you would never wish on people. They were both unexpected and extremely difficult times, but they played a massive part in shaping who he was a person.

> You never know where your next learning experience will come from, but it is important to know those experiences can help shape who you will be in the future.

You never know where your next learning experience will come from, but it is important to know those experiences can help shape who you will be in the future.

Your Learning Process

Your learning process is a continuous journey to becoming a better coach, and a better person. The elite 21st Century coach consistently looks for ways to improve their methods to improve themselves and their athletes.

Learning can take place in many different forms. Let's use an analogy about a laptop. People consistently upgrade the software on their laptops. They have identified the laptop can't do something, so they download some more stuff on to it. That's one element, and as coaches across the board we are good at downloading more stuff into our software department. We go on courses, we do continuous personal development, we read and observe others to add more software to what we already have. The problem can be when you add too much, the software on the computer slows down a little bit. Lots of coaches have their heads filled with information, or they're on twitter consistently

"The illiterate of the 21st Century will not be those who cannot read and write, but those who cannot learn, unlearn and relearn."
– Alvin Toffler

wanting to share their ideas, when really, they need to do a bit of a data dump. There are thousands of new ideas floating around, but simplicity may actually be the genius. Your job is not to overcomplicate the process. It is to make the process as simple and easy to understand as possible.

"Simplicity is the trademark of genius." – Robin Sharma

How often do you take time to clear stuff off your software to make sure your mind is not cluttered? If I said to you, you're really good on the laptop, but you're probably only using 20% of its capacity because it has too much going on, you would likely take out what isn't needed. A really good

> **"Simplicity is the trademark of genius."**
> **– Robin Sharma**

way to find out what is and is not needed is to reflect and look inwards. Use your experiences to find out what may, or may not work, reflect on the experiences and use it to your advantage next time.

"We do not learn from experience. We learn from reflecting on experience." – John Dewey

To become great at something you need to do it a lot, and honestly reflect on the experiences. Nick Marshall has been coaching for 27 years and spent a lot of them at the highest levels within English Academy football and is continually learning to honestly reflect. "As a coach you are like the athlete in the sense that you will both make mistakes. I've coached across all ages and all

> **"We do not learn from experience. We learn from reflecting on experience."**
> **– John Dewey**

levels of ability on my journey. I practiced and made loads of mistakes that I learned from. Reflecting on those mistakes is a great way to grow, as I'm still making them and I'm still learning from them!" said Nick.

Be honest and inquisitive when reflecting to really help you unlock your potential. If something can go better next time, how can it go better? If you have struggled to connect with an athlete, is that because of the athlete, or is that because of you? Spend more time looking at solutions and less time blaming the athlete for something that you could have helped with.

For Mick Beale on his road to being the most elite coach he possibly can, he quickly realised through his reflections that understanding cultures and languages were the higher level of coaching. Working across every age group from the youngest kids to adults in many different parts of England and Scotland and working in Sao Paolo in South America helped him learn and understand cultures. Mick believes it was massively important to learn about different cultures. Learning how life is seen differently can help give you a greater ability to build a connection with people within that culture.

"Understanding different cultures and languages is the real elite high-level learning of coaching," said Mick. "You have to tread carefully with other cultures and do your homework and observe in their environment. Once the message is sent you can't take it back so work hard to understand the culture so you can send the right messages." – Mick Beale.

Coaches also need to continue to learn from others because that will keep them moving in the right direction. It takes great courage to share your thoughts and get another person's thoughts to build another perspective on an athlete, rather than basing something entirely off what you think. Listen to other perspectives and see how experienced people work. You can't sit on your doorstep and expect it to happen, so it's important to put yourself in situations where you are able to get that.

Be Curious

"Successful people in all fields are all driven by curiosity. They are driven to do what they do better each time." – Richard Bandler

Curiosity is the urge to learn and acquire knowledge. Curious people ask questions, read and explore. They are active when it comes to seeking new information or experiences and are willing to meet challenges and to broaden their horizons.

Curiosity is important for excelling as a coach because you ask questions, learn from others, and look for ways to coach even more effectively. A curious mind is an active mind. It will put you in a better position to learn and coach better and more creatively.

Coaching is never an exact science, but it's important to check the

> "Successful people in all fields are all driven by curiosity. They are driven to do what they do better each time."
> – Richard Bandler

benefits of what you're doing and understanding if what you're currently doing outweighs changing your approach. Pete Sturgess believes

> "Optimal learning is driven by curiosity which leads to exploration, discovery, practice, and mastery. In turn, mastery leads to pleasure, satisfaction, and confidence to once again explore. The more a child experiences this cycle of wonder, the more she can create a lifelong excitement and love of learning. The cycle of wonder, however, can be stopped by fear."
> - Dr. Bruce D. Perry

if want to create curious athletes it is important; we are curious as coaches first. "If we want athlete's to be curious, but if I'm never curious about something I'm almost saying it isn't important."

To provide optimal learning environments, it is important to create curious environments. Dr. Bruce D. Perry, an American psychiatrist and expert in the field of child trauma said the following in his article Emotional Development: Creating an Emotionally Safe Classroom: "Optimal learning is driven by curiosity which leads to exploration, discovery, practice, and mastery. In turn, mastery leads to pleasure, satisfaction, and confidence to once again explore. The more a child experiences this cycle of wonder, the more she can create a lifelong excitement and love of learning. The cycle of wonder, however, can be stopped by fear." As a coach, creating curious learning environments that allow your athletes to explore and experiment can be very beneficial to the athlete's learnings.

"It's about having an attitude that has to do with curiosity, with wanting to know about things, wanting to be able to influence things, and wanting to be able to influence them in a way that's worthwhile." – Richard Bandler

Evolving and Adapting

Adaptability is a key to success. As coaches, we live in a rapidly changing world, and work in constantly changing sports, so we need to be able to adapt and evolve. People can get caught up in how they do things and be unwilling to change, but sports will leave them behind.

Justin Holbrook believes evolving, adapting and accepting change are some of the biggest things to becoming a 21st Century coach. Just like you are, the World is changing at a rapid pace. You may hear a grandparent comment about how they didn't sit around and watch TV when they were younger, but it's because they didn't have access to that technology. There is little point in saying 'we didn't play Fortnite as kids,' because Fortnite wasn't a thing.

"My message is to adapt with the changes, and don't try to shut the kids down because that's not what you did growing up," said Justin. "As a coach, don't look to ban everything. Kids have lives, and professionals have lives. Athletes have to make sacrifices but understand that they are more than just athletes. Make your athletes aware of the situation they are in in a good light. Yes, they can play fortnite, or watch TV, but for me, I make it clear that it's important to remember most people aren't fortunate enough to play first team rugby. There will be things athletes miss out on in life, but the rewards are great."

For Justin, one of the best ways of evolving is involving the players. For him, they're the ones going out playing. As much as you give messages out as the coach, it's down to the athlete's, so get their ideas as well. Justin believes it isn't solely about what he wants to do. Part of the way his teams play is based around having player input. If it makes them play better, then it's beneficial. He believes if a player is running out on to the pitch and is excited about the opportunities they're going to get as a player they're going to play better. If athlete's are going on to a pitch where the coach has told them 'they can only do this, and they can only do that,' it may last a certain amount of time, but athlete's tend to get bored with something they don't enjoy, so the relationship may not last long.

There are aspects of sports that don't go away and don't change. Hard work doesn't go away, but the way a sport is played may change. What worked 10 years ago may not work today, and what works today

> "As a coach, don't look to ban everything. Kids have lives, and professionals have lives. Athletes have to make sacrifices but understand that they are more than just athletes. Make your athletes aware of the situation they are in in a good light. Yes, they can play fortnite, or watch TV, but for me, I make it clear that it's important to remember most people aren't fortunate enough to play first team rugby. There will be things athletes miss out on in life, but the rewards are great."
>
> - Justin Holbrook

may not work in 10 years. It's important as coaches that we maintain principles that won't change and never will, but also being aware of principles that do change.

You hear people talking about the new school and old school coaches. It's the same school, and always has been the same school. You're just working with different athletes.

"A problem may arise within 'your school' when somebody says, 'in my day we didn't do that, or that's a poor attitude because you should be doing this,' said Ryan Maye. "In reality it's the same playground, there are just different kids playing in it. You have to listen and choose to invest the energy in the relationship."

> **You hear people talking about the new school and old school coaches. It's the same school, and always has been the same school. You're just working with different athletes.**

The planet leaves things behind that are not adaptable. Richard Dobson jokes with his players that the dinosaurs didn't adapt, and they became extinct. Mammals adapted over time, which is why they rule the Earth now. You have the ability to evolve and adapt. Take advantage of that.

Influence with Integrity

As a coach, you are in an exceptionally privileged position to influence people's lives. You therefore need to be very mindful of how you build relationships with athletes, coaches, parents and guardians. Insist that there is a transparency within your communication to your athletes. Make sure your colleagues and parents are aware of the processes being used with what you're doing, and how you're doing it.

Be clear on the level of relationship you're looking to build to really affect somebody's life. There will be a deepness, there will be an honesty and there will be a vulnerability that is often required to really impact peoples' lives. That can't be something that is just you and the athlete. It has to have multiple stakeholders to share with.

As a coach, you are in an exceptionally privileged position to influence people's lives.

Work with the person, then the athlete. Every coach will have some sort of technical skillset, and every coach can become more skilled around their sport. Build up the relationship with the person, then have enough depth and detail around the sport to make the relationship worthwhile for the athlete.

Understand the person behind the player. Influence the person and the athlete will follow. Richard Dobson hates that people in football clubs are just known as players. He had a player that had been injured for a long time and his career was in the balance. He got asked to speak at a convention and broke down while he was up in front of the crowd. He said at the convention 'I realised that I've always been defined as a footballer, and around my job. When

"The key thing is whilst you want them to do well and thrive in your working environment, there is a lot more to that person than just the player. Define them as people and as individuals first." – Richard Dobson

football was good, I had great self-esteem. When it wasn't good my self-esteem was really low. My identity has always been underpinned around me as a footballer. What I didn't realise was that football was one part of me. I'm also a boyfriend, a son, among many other things.'

When you approach every person on an individual basis and get to know them, you will have a better chance of getting to know them.

When you approach every person on an individual basis and get to know them, you will have a better chance of getting to know them.

Communicate Effectively

"The meaning of a communication is the result you get." – Richard Bandler

"It's easier to build strong children than it is to mend broken adults."
– Frederick Douglas

In Teaching Excellence, Richard Bandler describes the meaning of the communication as the response you get. In other words, if the way you are explaining something, or the way you are coaching is consistently not working, you may need to approach it from a different angle.

You do need knowledge in the sport you are involved in, but not as much as people may think. Some people are obsessed with tactics within sports, and bombarding people with messages, but you have to be able to communicate your message effectively with people first.

Steve Heighway believes a lot of peoples learning in life is done in retrospect. "Some things you tell your athlete today may not be learned on that day. That is why repetition of your message is so important. It's not about saying lots of things to tick boxes. It is about being clear, concise and consistent with your message over a period of time."

You have to hit home with your messages. When dealing with children, they're coming to you after being in a school environment where teachers may constantly talk. You may need to keep you message to a minimum but make it hard hitting with children.

The effective communicator is the coach that is clear and concise in what they want, allowing individuals to feel free within boundaries they set.

"You don't always need to know the encyclopaedia of something if you know how to manage and communicate with people." – Mick Beale.

"Some things you tell your athlete today may not be learned on that day. That is why repetition of your message is so important. It's not about saying lots of things to tick boxes. It is about being clear, concise and consistent with your message over a period of time."

"You don't always need to know the encyclopaedia of something if you know how to manage and communicate with people." – Mick Beale.

Utilise Your Mentors

Most top coaches across every sport have mentors and people they turn to for advice. Having people with vast experiences and wisdom around you to share what they have been through can help you become even better.

You've got to want to value mentors in your life. It's not to say you always have to have mentors around you. Anybody that doesn't want people around may not want them because that is where they are right now. They may not need it at that precise moment in time.

However, as a coach you only know what you know. Anybody can gather knowledge, and anybody can read or listen to a podcast. Being around people with a wealth of experience and a wealth of wisdom is something you cannot acquire overnight. Not just in sport, but outside of sport too.

For Justin Holbrook, he is a strong believer in talking to older people. "They've lived it," he said. "There are things about their life that you can learn. Back in Australia I've become good friends with a guy older than me. He started off owning one pub and is now the biggest hotel owner in Australia. Getting to know where he started from, and how he did it, and building a connection with him around his life is great."

"I love interesting people. I love reading books. Learn as much as you can. You can get something from most conversations, even if it's watching your kids football game. You could end up talking to a parent or grandparent and learn something about them. It doesn't mean the story has to have a good ending, but you can still take something from it and refer back to your own team. I share those stories, and reference it back to my players."

Justin told of a story about a guy in St. Helens who was a top U16 player at the club some years back who didn't end up making it as a professional. Justin told his players about the guy's story and related it back to what they were doing as a group. It was very fitting, and worked well in context, but had Justin not been open minded, he may have missed that learning opportunity.

Kevin Harper bounces off other coaches within the fighting game to seek advice on certain topics. There is a guy who runs a gym in Leeds who he has been friends with for years. It's probably the most successful gym there has ever been in Britain, and Kevin chats with the owner if he has questions he may not know.

He also enjoys speaking to people within other sports because they may have other views that could shed some light on how they can improve?

Whether it is somebody you trust implicitly, or whether it is somebody you look to for advice, valuing the grey hairs is important when striving to become the best coach you can possibly be.

Chapter 12 - The Conclusion – Be Like The Master Boilermaker

As coaches, we want to make a great difference to our athletes. How much do we look in the mirror and look at our role in the performance of our athletes? What can we do differently to further enhance the athletes experience, and how do we do that? We are in a privileged position to have an impact on their lives. As coaches, are we ensuring the impact we have is a positive one?

The Boilermaker Story

This book is not designed to be a quick fix. Coaching is a process of continual learning and growth, and this book has been written to help you along that path. Having knowledge is great, but the magic lies in when, where and how you use that knowledge. How do you do "the what?"

There is an old story of a boilermaker who was hired to fix a huge steamship boiler system that was not working well. After listening to the engineer's description of the problems and asking a few questions, he went to the boiler room.

He looked at the maze of twisting pipes, listened to the thump of the boiler and the hiss of the escaping steam for a few minutes, and felt some pipes with his hands. Then he hummed softly to himself, reached into his overalls and took out a small hammer, and tapped a bright red valve one time. Immediately, the entire system began working perfectly, and the boilermaker went home.

When the steamship owner received a bill for one thousand dollars, he became outraged and complained that the boilermaker had only been in the engine room for fifteen minutes and requested an itemized bill.

The boilermaker sent him a bill that reads as follows:

- For tapping the valve: $0.50
- For knowing when and where to tap: $999.50
- Total: $1,000.00

Lots of coaches can and do "tap the valve," but very few coaches know precisely when and where to "tap the valve." Become the master of knowing when and where to use your skills and techniques and know why you are doing it.

Be the highly effective coach that sets yourself out from the crowd. Be the highly effective coach that makes the differences that makes a difference in your athletes lives.

> Lots of coaches can and do "tap the valve," but very few coaches know precisely when and where to "tap the valve." Become the master of knowing when and where to use your skills and techniques and know why you are doing it.

The foundations, skills, techniques, and behaviours within the book are to create a greater awareness of how to coach more effectively, and to give you an insight of when and where to "tap the valve." This book identifies ways to coach and communicate more effectively. It is not the only way.

> "I've learned that people may forget what you said, people may forget what you did, but people will never forget how you made them feel."
> – Maya Angelou

Coaching is a continually evolving field, but there is a vapor trail behind successful people. It's important to model and copy what is already working, while bringing your own personality and authentic approach to the table. Listen to what other people have to say, learn from those around you, and enrich the people you come into contact with. Pay more attention to the finer details around you and tune in to those special moments. The differences that make the difference in what it is you do.

It's important to remember:

"I've learned that people may forget what you said, people may forget what you did, but people will never forget how you made them feel."
– Maya Angelou

Along with those who directly contributed to the book, there are many other people who have helped us on our journey.

In particular, we would like to extend our sincerest thankyou's to the following people for their help and advice with proof reading and finalising the book:

Andrew Norman, who attended an FA Level 4 Psychology Course Keith delivered. He has been professional experience in the fields of psychology, business and sports coaching, was a BBC broadcaster, and was a professional proof-reader for over 12 years.

George Collins, who is a very dear friend and mentor that we both trust implicitly. He has experiences in the business fields, operating as CEO and COO in multi-million-dollar businesses.

John LaValle, who has become a good friend of ours after we participated on the NLP courses he delivered. John is the President of the society of NLP. He is one of the world's most respected corporate consultants and co-authored 'Persuasion Engineering' with Dr. Richard Bandler.

"Wow, what a great read. Powerful stuff. I learned a lot!" – Andrew Norman

"One hell of a job. A really solid read!" – George Collins

"Loads of success with this book. I think it's fab!" – John LaValle

About The Authors

As two ex-soccer players who represented professional clubs, David and Keith Mayer both followed similar paths in their playing careers. They both played in England, and David played in Spain. Both David and Keith had relatively successful college careers in America. David was a two-year captain at a #1 ranked Division 1 school, while Keith captained a winning National Championship team and was named MVP in 1982. They both suffered very similar injuries throughout their careers, both retiring at young ages.

After retiring from playing, both David and Keith started coaching. Keith became one of the youngest UEFA A License coaches in England at the time, passing in 1985. Keith was mentored by and was a close friend of one of the greatest coach educators of all time, Dick Bate. Keith worked alongside Dick, presenting on Pro License courses, among other things.

Keith has coached ex England Internationals while working at three highly successful Academies in England and is currently coaching at Liverpool FC's prestigious Academy. Keith is also currently an FA Affiliate Tutor and delivered on the FA Level 4 Psychology course.

He has been a National Team Head Coach on an interim basis for one of England's National Teams and was the Head Coach for England U20's Cerebral Palsy Team on their winning trip to Brazil in 2013.

Keith has personally mentored Premier League Footballers, England National Team Coaches, a Pride of Britain Winner, a World Champion athlete, a PGA Golfer, an Assistant Manager of a Football League Club in England, personnel within soccer in America, personnel within the South Korean Football Association and many more. Keith is highly respected across the world for his work, delivering on six continents.

Keith's credentials and experiences where valuable for David on his journey as a coach. For David, being able to get guidance, and observe some of the finest coach educators in the world not only helped him understand the time, organisation and fine details that go into being elite, but also enabled him to gain invaluable experiences to continue to help his progression as a person. David's upbringing was distinctive and provided a platform that most others would not receive.

David is currently completing his UEFA A License, expected June 2020, and was an Assistant Coach at the National Champion Pfeiffer University Soccer Team and Manchester City Football Schools. He has also coached and delivered on four continents and has recently accepted a position to become the Global Head of Foundation Phase for a club based out of Utah called 7Elite Academy.

Both David and Keith are NLP Master Practitioners, which helped shape their values and beliefs, and in turn greatly helped the athletes they have worked with. Their combined knowledge and desire to help athletes have better experiences led David and Keith to write this book.

References

Bandler, R., & Benson, K. (2018). *Teaching Excellence: The Definitive Guide to NLP for Teaching and Learning*. [S.l.]: New Thinking Publications.

Carnegie, D. (1936). *How To Win Friends and Influence People*. Simon and Schuster.

Krzyzweski, C., & Phillips, D. (2011). *Leading with the Heart: Coach K's Successful Strategies for Basketball, Business, and Life*. Grand Central Publishing.

Dweck, C. (2007). The Perils and Promises of Praise. *Educational Leadership*, *65*(2), 34-39. Retrieved from http://www.ascd.org

Interview with Kung Fu Panda director John Stevenson. (2015, January 25). Retrieved from http://www.animationxpress.com/index.php/interviews/interview-with-kung-fu-panda-director-john-stevenson

Perry, B. D. (n.d.). Emotional Development: Creating an Emotionally Safe Classroom. Retrieved from https://www.scholastic.com/teachers/articles/teaching-content/emotional-development-creating-emotionally-safe-classroom/.

Printed in Poland
by Amazon Fulfillment
Poland Sp. z o.o., Wrocław

51260655R00085